MEMORY
MADE *EASY*

MEMORY
MADE *EASY*
The Complete Book of Memory Training

ROBERT L. MONTGOMERY

A Division of American Management Associations

Library of Congress Cataloging in Publication Data

Montgomery, Robert Leo, 1927–
  Memory made easy.

   1. Mnemonics. I. Title.
BF385.M87   153.1'4   79-10889
ISBN 0-8144-5523-9

Third Printing

Contents

MEMORY MADE *EASY*

1
Memory Improvement: An Introduction

FIRST, A LITTLE HISTORY

Thirteen years ago, archaeologists working in the Middle East discovered a remarkable pictograph created by an early human culture. The carvings, made on clay-like mud that was then allowed to harden, showed recognizable constellations along with human figures and farming equipment. In February 1976, at the Explorers Club in New York City, one of the archaeologists who had been studying the pictograph revealed his findings. The carvings, which date from 2500 B.C., reveal that these early humans

1

used the picture method—pictures of stars plus pictures of a plow plus pictures of people—to remember when to plant and when to plow. So today, when we try to remember something the easy way, by using mental pictures, we are using a system similar to one created by a civilization existing more than 4,000 years ago!

The Greeks and Romans both devised unique picture-association systems to help them remember lists of ideas or important data. They visualized each item or idea in its own spot in a different room of the home. For example, to remember to buy gold, incense, and myrrh, they might picture gold in the living quarters of the home, incense in the dining area, and myrrh in the sleeping room. They knew what we know today: that a vivid association can make possible almost instant recall of any list any time, even years later. Memory, after all, is defined in the dictionary as "the mental capacity or faculty of retaining and reviving impressions, or of recalling or recognizing previous experiences."

THE BRAIN: YOUR PERSONAL COMPUTER

What about the marvelous machine that makes all this possible? Over the centuries, man has created endless wonders, but nothing that even approximates the miracle of the human brain. It is the most magnificent bit of miniaturization in the universe. It weighs only three pounds, and yet it contains some eleven billion nerve cells, each having some twenty-five thousand possible interconnections with other nerve cells. I'm often asked if computers will ever replace this super-machine, the brain. A computer large enough to provide the same range of choice would require an area equal to the entire surface of the earth!

Because of its complexity and flexibility, because it responds to training much as a muscle does, your brain's capacity to remember can actually be increased by three to four hundred percent. All that's necessary is that you master the techniques in this book. And you can—*if* you work hard enough at it. Thousands of people have done it before you. Many of them have gone on to become experts. Some lecture, others write. As a matter of fact, a great many books and cassettes on memory have been released in just the last few years. *Remembering the Word,* by former professional basketball star Jerry Lucas, even tells how to memorize the Bible using picture associations!

The methods you learn in this book will show you why I chose the title. Memory will be easy, believe me. Effectiveness in remembering simply depends on skills *that can be learned.* If you need proof, think this over. Policemen trained in reporting their observations did better at memory and observation tests than did Phi Beta Kappa college seniors who had had no training.

WHAT GOOD IS A GOOD MEMORY?

No matter what walk of life you're in, a well-developed memory is bound to be of incalculable value. In business particularly, one of the most irritating problems, and one of the costliest, is forgetfulness. The busy manager's most immediate need is a reliable memory. But whoever you are, I promise you that once you've mastered the essentials in this book, you will enjoy some remarkable benefits. A good memory can give you greater peace of mind. If that sounds hard to believe—wouldn't it relieve you to know that you can remember a client's casual request, a new customer's name, your mother-in-law's message to your mate? I can also promise you greater confidence—the assurance that comes from having a dependable memory for the names, the facts, the dates we all have to cope with every day. Your new ability to recall data, to bring up important facts, can help you achieve greater stature in business, and may even help you get that promotion. Finally, you're bound to be a more interesting conversationalist. Watch your friends and co-workers respond when you remember, with no trouble at all, people's names, interesting facts about them, details of the day's news, unusual data about books and shows and sports events.

In Cervantes' *Don Quixote,* the hero, the Man of La Mancha, says: "My memory is so bad that many times I forget my own name." If things sometimes seem almost that bad, relax! Remembering names will be easy for you once you master the following techniques.

HOW TO BEGIN

In Lewis Carroll's *Alice in Wonderland,* the king remarks at one point: "The horror of that moment, I shall never forget it!" "You will, though," says the queen, "if you don't make a memorandum of it."

Writing down whatever you want to recall later is a good practice any time, but especially for those new to memory-building. First, you will have a record of names, facts, and expenses when you need them. After all, would you trust yourself to remember the expense you must report to the Internal Revenue Service? Even more important: what you need most of all is to develop a second-nature, almost subconscious reaction that lets you *associate new data* for instant recall later. And seeing a fact, jokes, names, or numbers makes a more lasting impression than hearing it. Later you'll learn tricks for remembering without writing. But for now—write it down! Even though I've trained my memory in all the ways I'll be teaching you, I've made it a practice for years to carry three-by-five cards in my pocket and in my briefcase so I can jot down names, promises, quotations, agreements, dates, appointments, ideas, and even an occasional poem. Some of the material I'm using in this book is still preserved just as I wrote it on those cards. I've used the material in teaching, and I've made cassettes of it. If I hadn't written down all those items, chances are I'd never have remembered some of them. I even write down the jokes I hear! Once I've used them a few times, I can trust my memory. If we never really learn something in the first place, it's impossible to recall it.

Before I get down to explaining the principles of memory and the systems and techniques that make remembering easy, I want to give you a sample of what it's like to learn a long list of items. We'll go into it more deeply later; right now, I just want you to see how much fun it can be. If you listen carefully and concentrate as we go along, you'll probably be surprised at how well you do— even *before* we start the serious work.

All set? Then visualize these items as I describe them.

First, picture in your mind's eye an expensive china plate on the floor in front of you. Delicate chinaware.

Second, jammed into the delicate chinaware is a huge fountain pen. The giant pen has been driven right into the center of the plate and is sticking out of it, and the delicate chinaware is cracked. Third, perched on top of the huge pen there's a new calf, a jersey calf. You can hear it mooing. On the calf, whirling around like a cowboy, sits King George of England dressed in royal red robes and sporting a long cut on his cheek. Connecting the ends of the cut is a big Band-Aid.

Take pencil and paper now and try to write down the first five objects. Let's review them.

> On the floor there's a plate; delicate chinaware.
> Jammed into it is a huge fountain pen.
> On the pen there's a jersey calf—a new calf.
> Sitting on the calf is King George.
> He has a Band-Aid connecting the ends of the cut on his cheek.

Now let's add some more objects. On top of King George's head there's a mass of ice, a solid mass of ice in block form.

Sitting on the ice is a beautiful woman named Marilyn. In her lap there's an ocean liner and it's pointed south. You know it's pointed south because the ice is melting and it's running down King George's face. There's just one smokestack on the ocean liner. And packed into the top of the smokestack you see a big ham. It's a new ham.

6

Now let's review. Again, try to write down the first nine items.

What's on the floor? And jammed into it is a huge _____? What's on the pen? And what's on top of the calf? And what's on his face? And on his head is—? And sitting on the ice is—? And what's in her lap? And what's on the smokestack?

Let's stack a few more objects and see how we do.

You look through binoculars and see that the new ham in the smokestack is wrapped in a song sheet. You can read the title: "Carry Me Back to Old Virginny."

Now you can also see something else. Standing on the ham and reaching high into the sky is a gigantic replica of the Empire State Building. It's on top of the ham, pushing the new ham down into the smokestack.

You note that on top of the Empire State Building there's a weather vane in the form of an ocean liner, and it's pointing north.

Let's see how you're doing. Going back to Marilyn sitting on the mass of ice on King George's head: what's in Marilyn's lap? Which way is the first ocean liner headed? And what's stuck in the smokestack of the ocean liner? And what's it wrapped in? And on top of it, what do we see? And at the top of the Empire State Building is—what? Headed in which direction? Sure; the higher you go into the air, the colder it is. So it's pointing north. Now let's add one more object. On the deck of the ocean liner there's a hen, a Rhode Island Red. She's just laid an egg, and is cackling away.

There you have thirteen objects. Can you recall all of

7

them? Before you read further, try to write down the thirteen items in the same order I gave them to you.

How did you do? Not bad! Now, I told you this list would have practical value, and here's what I mean. What you have just learned are the names of the thirteen original colonies in the order in which they joined the union. You learned by picturing, stacking, and linking the objects together.

The first object was *delicate chinaware*. What state would that be? Right! Delaware. And what's jammed into the plate? So what state came next? That's it, *Penn*sylvania. Good thing we're all used to nicknames! And what state is represented by the *new* calf? Of course. We said it was a *new* calf and a *jersey* calf. What's the fourth state of the union? New Jersey! King *George* reminds us naturally of Georgia. And remember the cut on his face? And we said that *connecting* the ends of the *cut* was a Band-Aid. Have you figured out the fifth state? Connecticut. And on King George's head was a *mass* of ice. The state is? Yes, Massachusetts. Got the idea? Easy, isn't it. Now—can you guess the last seven states of the union from the objects we stacked? Who's sitting on the mass of ice on King George's head? Just her first name gives the state—Maryland. And on *Marilyn's* lap pointed *south* is an *ocean liner*. What's the state? Yes! South Carolina.

And jammed into the smokestack is what? And the state is? *New Ham*pshire. New ham. And the *new ham* is wrapped in a song sheet. What state does it represent? Virginia. And state number eleven is next. The building perched on the new ham is the symbol of the state, the

Empire State Building. New York, of course. And the weather vane at the top pointing north tells us the twelfth state. Remember, it was an *ocean liner* pointed *north*. North Carolina. And on the deck of the ship, a *Rhode Island* Red hen laid an egg, and is cackling. We could have her cackle thirteen times, or lay thirteen eggs to remember our thirteenth state, Rhode Island.

There you have them, the thirteen original colonies in the order in which they joined the union. If you review the stack of objects and the states a few times, you'll find it impossible to forget. Later, I'll explain in detail the stack-and-link technique and its many uses, but before we do that, we'll have to learn the basic principles of remembering, as well as some essential prerequisites.

One final thought about the thirteen colonies. Whenever I do this, someone always comes up and asks, "O.K., but do you know which state was the *fourteenth* to join?" Just so you'll know when someone asks *you,* the answer is Vermont. To remember the fourteenth state, picture a plastic bottle of Vermont Maid syrup as the item the Rhode Island Red hen laid. And picture the syrup dripping down over the entire stack of objects. Vermont syrup.

2
How to Remember: Some Fundamental Principles

THE PREREQUISITES

Most of us, psychologists say, don't use more than 10 percent of our native ability to remember. That's comparable to running a car on one or two cylinders and just poking along.

Why don't we use more of our inherent memory power? There are several answers. First, because we haven't been trained to. Nowhere in our schooling were we taught how to use our powers of memory. And second, because we often just don't *care*. And that leads me to the three things that I feel are essential to a more powerful memory.

First, you must have a burning *desire* to improve your memory. *You must care about it.* Most people struggle along with poor memories, enduring endless frustrations and embarrassments in their daily lives, because they just don't want to be bothered remembering the constant barrage of names, numbers, facts, and information. What you have to do is remind yourself of the many benefits of a good memory: the increased confidence I promised you, the popularity, the peace of mind. Aren't those three alone enough to stir a desire in you to improve?

The second prerequisite is the ability to *concentrate.* You will be effective in remembering to the degree that you care enough to concentrate. A short period of intense concentration will often enable you to accomplish more than years of dreaming.

The third prerequisite was revealed to me by former Postmaster-General James Farley of New York City. Mr. Farley was cited by associates for having the most remarkable memory in this century. I asked him his secret.

"There's no real secret," he said. "You simply must *love people.* If you do, you won't have any trouble remembering their names, and a lot more about them than that."

And that's the third essential: You must *care about people.* It wasn't long after I talked to Mr. Farley that I came across an interesting line from Alexander Pope. "How vast a memory has love," he wrote. Certainly a deeper interest in people, and in your work as well, should make your desire to remember and your concentration much easier.

12

THE BASIC LAWS

Visualize

Now you're ready to learn the basic techniques for developing your memory. The first essential is to *visualize*. Picture what you want to remember. Since 85 percent of all you learn and remember in life reaches you through your eyes, it is absolutely vital that you visualize the things you want to recall later. To do that, you must above all become *aware*. And awareness involves becoming both a keen observer and an active listener. You have to see clearly and hear accurately in order to picture vividly what you want to remember. Too many people go through life only partly awake, only partly aware. They don't forget names; they never hear them clearly in the first place. The art of *retention* is the art of *attention*.

Become curious, observant, and sensitive to everything around you. See the roof detail on that old building. Notice the difference between the tree greens of April and of August. Hear the difference between the sirens of an ambulance, a fire truck, a police car. Sharpen your senses of sight and hearing—they're the most important. Together, those two senses account for 95 percent of our memory power. Two ancient sayings highlight the importance of visualizing. "One time seeing is worth a thousand times hearing." And "A picture is worth ten thousand words."

Repeat

If school didn't bother to teach us formal memory work, it did teach us the need for *repeating*. We were taught to

13

memorize by repeating a poem, a date, or the alphabet over and over again. Radio and television commercials rely heavily on repetition to remind listeners to buy, buy, buy.

Is there an American who doesn't recognize "Try it, you'll like it" or "I can't believe I ate the whole thing"? Burger King's famous "Have it your way" moved Mc-Donald's, who got busy and created the line, "You, you're the one." When slogans like these are set to music, people don't just remember them—they even sing them. And there you have the secret of success: repetition.

Associate

Before we get into actual demonstrations of the kinds of memory and the application of techniques, there's one more key to memory, and it's the most important. The one indispensable fundamental is the requirement that you *associate* anything you want to recall later. Association is the natural as well as the easy way to assure instant recall. Your brain is more remarkable than even the most amazing computer in the world. And the principle on which it works is association. The brain is, in fact, an associating machine. To recall a name, date, or fact, what the brain needs is a cue, a clue.

Let's step back into history for a moment. Over 2,000 years ago Aristotle defined what he called the Primary Laws of Association. There is the Law of Resemblance or Similarity, where one impression tends to bring to mind another impression which resembles it in some way. There is the Law of Contrast or Opposites, which says that where

14

there are two or more opposing impressions, the presence of one will tend to recall the others. And finally there is the Law of Contiguity or Togetherness. If two or more impressions occur at the same time, or follow close on one another in either time or space, thinking of one will recall the other.

There are secondary Laws of Association as well, and these are known as Recency, Frequency, and Vividness. *Recency* means we tend to recall associations made recently much better than those made months or years ago. *Frequency* implies that the more often you repeat an association, the easier it will be to recall. And *vividness* means that the more graphic or striking the association is, the quicker you'll be able to recall it. You'll see how these three laws apply as we go through our lessons.

In summary, the requirements for improving your memory are concentration, a desire to remember, and a love for people.

And the techniques for mastering the art of memory are visualizing, repeating, and associating.

One final note, this time on how to study: Memorizing anything is easier and faster when you practice for a half hour or so, and then go off and forget it for a while. Work again later for another half hour, then take another break. Tests have proved time and again that we learn better and faster when we alternate work and rest in a sort of wave pattern. The rest period actually reinforces the learning.

Now then, can you remember all that?

Let's get busy and learn how!

3
How to
Remember Names

VISUALIZE, REPEAT, ASSOCIATE!

Remembering the names of people you meet is easy when you practice the fundamentals we've just covered. Listening, clarifying, thinking, repeating, and then establishing a helpful association—those are the principles, and I'll demonstrate how to live up to them. But *you'll* have to do the work. *You'll* have to practice making your own associations, repeating, and visualizing. And the more you practice all three techniques, the easier it will be to recall names instantly.

17

When you meet someone for the first time, it's important to hear the name correctly. Ask for the correct spelling. Verify the pronunciation. Ask about the nationality, and find out whether the last name has a special meaning. Use the name immediately in conversation, particularly the last name. Repeat the name as you get acquainted; even repeating it silently to yourself will help you remember it correctly years later. And write it down as soon as you can. (Don't forget: 85 percent of what you remember comes through your eyes.) Here's an example of how it all works:

"Hi there, I'm Bob Montgomery."

"Hello! I'm Kay Tcholakian."

"Kay Tcholakian, nice to meet you. How do you spell your name?"

"T-c-h-o-l-a-k-i-a-n. Tcholakian."

"Where are you from, Miss Tcholakian?"

"I'm from Israel."

"Do you work here in New York City?"

"Yes, my brothers have a photography shop, and I work as the receptionist."

"Again, nice meeting you, Miss Tcholakian. Good luck!"

In a matter of seconds I heard her name five times and I got her to spell it for me. So in short order I've understood it and I know how to spell it. Now, how to associate it so I'll fix it indelibly in my mind?

AN EASY WAY TO REMEMBER: RHYME!

My favorite association technique is rhyming. I never forget anything I can manage to rhyme. Obviously, rhyming isn't always possible, but it's the trick I try first. In fact, I've made up a rhyme to help us recall the name we just learned together. "Kay Tcholakian is not Slovakian." Naturally not. She's Israeli—she told us so herself. It should be easy to spell the name and also to recall it. The more of these associations you make, the easier it becomes.

You're probably nodding away there, recalling how easy it was to remember what you learned in school once you used a rhyme. Sometimes your teacher provided the rhyme: "Thirty days hath September, April, June, and November. All the rest have thirty-one, except February, which has twenty-eight, and in leap year, twenty-nine." I didn't have to look that one up; I've remembered it ever since grade school. Another rhyme comes back to me from English class: "*I* before *E* except after *C*, or when sounded like *A*, as in neighbor or weigh." The point is, rhymes make information unforgettable, and names after all are information.

If you can tie the individual's job to the rhyme, you've got an easy way to remember more than just the name. Years ago I met a man named Tony Gohl, which rhymed with goal. He worked for the telephone company and he was about six feet four inches tall. I made up a quick little rhyme: "Tony's Gohl is a telephone pole." And I've never forgotten either his name or the fact that he works for the phone company.

DRAW MENTAL PICTURES

Probably the most reliable method of remembering names by association is simply to make a mental picture of

19

the name plus the person it attaches to. Remember: *visualize*.

And that brings up three important rules for becoming an *ACE* at remembering names—or, for that matter, any combination of facts or ideas you're trying to remember. A stands for Action. Get some action into the picture, and always try to get involved in the action. For example, there's a fellow I know named John Ford. I picture him shaking hands with former President Ford. Again, the A of ACE is for Action. Build it into your mental picture. Get yourself involved in some way if you can; get into the action if possible.

The C of ACE is for Color, the colors of the rainbow. In our television era we've all become accustomed to color. So capitalize on our awareness of color whenever you can. If you meet someone with red hair, build that into the association. Try to make color a part of whatever picture you invent.

E is for Exaggeration. The more ridiculous, the more ludicrous, the more exaggerated you can make your mental pictures, the better they'll help you remember.

When I taught you how to remember the original thirteen colonies, I purposely put Action, Color, and Exaggeration into the pictures. I made the ocean liner smaller, the hen red, the pen huge, King George whooping it up seated on a calf whirling around on a pen stuck in a plate. It's the action, the color, the sense of the ridiculous that make you an ACE at remembering, and that can often produce astonishing results.

In looking through my address book right now, I'll pick

a few people at random and give you the pictures I'd use to remember their last names. You can use my associations if you find they're helpful. But it's better to make up your own; they'll stick with you longer. Just grab the first crazy idea your mind throws at you. And remember: Action! Color! Exaggeration!

Here's an insurance man, Doug Hyer. I picture him on tiptoe with his hand high in the air. He's waving at me frantically, and in that waving hand is a check for me. He can't get any *higher* than his tiptoes, and I hope the check is for a *high* amount. And he's such an enthusiastic salesman, I would *hire* him to work for me. With all that in one picture, I remember Doug Hyer. I recall his first name by figuring he dug down deep in his pocket to bring me a refund check. That's Doug Hyer, and that's how I remember his name.

Lola Bishop is an agent in New York. I picture her as a woman bishop, wearing a miter and giving a blessing. I'm in the congregation as the collection is passed, and it occurs to me that whatever Lola wants, Lola gets. Both names leap up whenever I see that picture.

Here's a cousin of mine, Joe Hock, a retired accountant. Not that I need a device to remember a cousin! But if I did, I'd visualize him with a big coffeepot, going into a hock shop to get money for it. But first he's pouring a cup of coffee, a cup of joe for all, including myself. One American nickname for coffee, for some reason, is "joe," and the hock shop provides the last name.

Beth Green is a friend, and it's fun to picture her mowing the green grass with green backs—dollar bills, thousands of them, flying out of the mower and whirling all over. I'm shouting, "Beth, Beth! You're mowing green bills." How can you forget her? Beth Green.

Helen Grant I picture as General Grant giving me orders to take a message to Helen of Troy. I visualize her in the uniform of a general, and I see myself saluting her. Again, wherever I can, I try to associate both the first and last names.

Joe Jankowski I picture astride a cow. The cow is on skis, and Joe is saying, "Giddyup, Jan!" I see Joe's cowboy hat fly off and I holler, "Whoa, Joe!" Action and exaggeration again—I try to build them into every visual. And because it's important to add some color, I make the cow brown and white. The name again? Joe Jankowski. As usual, I spell it out carefully: J-a-n-k-o-w-s-k-i.

Are you getting the idea? Were you able to think of pictures of your own instead of the ones I suggested? Before long, you'll find associations popping into your mind like magic. For most names, I find I can come up with an instant idea, and I grab it—the best one is usually the one I think of first. Also, I feel it's important for quick and accurate recall of a name that we make the association as close to the actual pronunciation as possible. For example, I met an attorney named Tom Drake. I immediately thought, "Tom Drake can bake a cake." I pictured him in a chef's hat mixing the dough. It may sound silly, but it makes accurate recall magically easy!

I've always been at a disadvantage in remembering names because my own name is so easy for people to recall. All through the years I was growing up, there was that famous movie star. While I was starting in business, he was doing his own TV show, "Robert Montgomery Presents." And he went on from there to become speech consultant for President Eisenhower. It was a popular name, and so it was simple for people to remember me. (Just as well I got started on memory training early, so I could learn to remember them!)

The point is that you're at a distinct advantage when you meet someone with a famous name, or with the name of someone you know. Just visualize the two people shaking hands and you'll associate those identical last names from then on. (Obviously, it's the last name, the surname, that's the more important one to remember. Try finding Ray or Nancy in the phone directory!)

Some people's names are easy to recall because they have definite meanings. I once knew a man named Bob Rock. Rock is easy, you say; it has a literal meaning in nature, a part of mother earth. Still, I suggest you invent a visualization, or find some even stronger association, to be sure you remember. Bob Rock was a salesman and I used to picture him throwing rocks at me when I wouldn't buy his product. I haven't seen him in twenty years, but I can't forget his name.

By the way, the rhymes you make up and the mental pictures you create are your own secrets. Sometimes I make up associations that are so ridiculous I'd never want to tell the person involved. Occasionally I tell someone how I remember his or her name, but never when my little invention would embarrass or hurt the person involved.

When I first learned formal memory techniques thirty

years ago, I found it easy to make mental associations based on the person's appearance. For instance, Martha Booth was so huge, I had only to picture her trying to squeeze into a telephone booth. Exaggerating the visual, I pictured her jammed in the door and struggling to get out. That picture provided her surname, Booth, the moment I saw her.

Unfortunately, visuals based on appearances aren't too reliable these days. Women wear wigs of all shapes; some have wardrobes of wigs in different colors as well. And men wear hair pieces; or they sprout mustaches and beards that change their images, or they wear hats that alter their looks drastically. Diets are a fad today, and people can lose a great deal of weight virtually overnight. How many people do you know who've disappeared, and returned with a nose job? The list of entertainers who've done just that is endless. And think how many different styles of clothes we wear today! So be careful when establishing a mental picture based on appearance.

There are some physical types that do remain constant, however, and a few examples may be helpful. I met a lovely young lady named Pat Olson. I spelled it out for myself: O-l-s-o-n, not Ol-sen. She looked so pretty and healthy, I used a rhyme based on appearance: "Pat Olson is wholesome." For assurance, I added, "Ol's daughter, not Ol's son." For good-looking Ken Hanson (I spelled it to myself, H-a-n-s-o-n), I used an appearance-rhyme: "Ken Hanson is handsome." Cecilia Brown is a student I met in one of my classes, a nice girl with big brown eyes.

24

I pictured her as a singer, belting out "Beautiful Brown Eyes." For good measure, I also picture her singing the song "Cecilia." Hard to forget either of her names—or the color of her eyes!

Perhaps these things sound silly to you, or difficult to do. I assure you it will become easier and easier if you keep following my suggestions and principles, if you keep working at it every time you meet someone new. Also, the more ridiculous the association, the better the system will work for you. Since all the exaggeration is purely mental, no one need ever know how silly your imagination can get. And I promise you, for our purposes—the sillier, the better!

It's also true that once you improve your memory in one category, such as names, you'll find you have a better memory for all sorts of other things. Besides an improved ability to recall, you can count on a surge of confidence that will strengthen your personality. There's another side benefit, too: the time you'll save by *not* having to rummage through files, notebooks, or phone books. I occasionally forget to take my glasses with me, but I always remember where I left them. My hand has been trained to see and recall.

LET'S TAKE THE REPETITION TEST

It's time to put *you* to work now. You're going to start applying the principles we've been discussing, and we'll see how they help you in learning a variety of names.

Let's introduce you to a few new people, and see if you

25

can remember their names. Here comes a pleasant fellow.
"My name is Ralph Raitt. That's spelled R-a-i-t-t.
Rhymes with rate."

Alright, first crack out of the box; spell his last name out
loud: Raitt, R-a-i-t-t. Next, since the genial gentleman is
bald, think of the rhyme, "Ralph Raitt has a bald pate."
Let's use it. "Ralph Raitt has a bald pate." O.K., now
you say it:

"Ralph Rate has a bald pate."

Here's a pretty lady.

"My name is Katie Lyback. That's spelled L-y-
b-a-c-k."

Let's all spell the name: L-y-b-a-c-k. Her full name is
Katie Lyback. K-K-K-Katie like the song. We can picture
her lying back on a hammock singing K-K-K-Katie. Can
you visualize that scene? Almost enough to revive the
song, isn't it? Now shut your eyes and play it all back.

Who was the first gentleman we met?

And what's the name of the lady we met next?

LET'S TAKE THE ASSOCIATION TEST

Let's work with some more names.

"I'm Louis Dockswell. I work on Wall Street as a
broker and my name is spelled just as it sounds—
D-o-c-k-s-w-e-l-l."

"Let's spell his name out loud: Dockswell; D-o-c-k-s-
w-e-l-l. His first name is? Louis. His full name? Louis
Dockswell.

Let's picture him in a skipper's cap docking his motor-
boat at the foot of Wall Street. We note how expertly he

26

docks the boat and we tell ourselves that Louis sure *docks well*. You could say *Lou is* a fine skipper. Again, his full name is?

What is the lady doing as she *lies back* in the hammock? Right! Singing K-K-K-Katie. And her last name is?

What is the last name of the fellow who has a bald pate? Raitt. Right! And his full name is?

Here's another.

"My name is Colleen Butler. I'm a receptionist for an advertising agency. My name is spelled B-u-t-l-e-r."

An attractive Colleen with a surname right out of the servant's quarters in some elegant home. I picture her in a butler's formal dark suit, greeting me at the door with the butler's formal question: "May I say who is calling, please?" Should be easy to recall a female butler! Well, let's see if you can.

What's her last name? And what's her full name?

And Ralph with the bald pate. What's his last name?

What's the name of the lady in the hammock?

What's the name of the skipper who's mooring his boat?

And what's the last name of the Colleen greeting us at the door?

You're doing so well, let's add a few more names to our test. Practice is the best instructor.

"I am Gloria Betancourt. I'm a housewife and the mother of two children. My name is spelled B-e-t-a-n-c-o-u-r-t."

And it's pronounced? Bet-an-court. Her first name is? Gloria. Can you see her in a courtroom making a bet? Gloria *bet in court* that she would be found not guilty. And

27

what a glorious day when she was declared not guilty! You should visualize both you and Gloria in that courtroom making that bet. Got it? Now—her last name is? Betancourt. First name? Gloria. Full name? Gloria Betancourt.

Get a vivid picture, the most ridiculous picture possible, to be sure the name will stick. And always try to put yourself in that picture. Get involved. It makes instant recall just that much more certain. Be sure to repeat the name as much as possible. Use it in conversation; go over it silently as well. Let's review again:

> Who's docking his boat?
> Who's in the hammock?
> Who has the bald pate?
> What's the name of the Colleen meeting us at the front door?
> And who's putting money on the table in court?

One more and we'll see how many you can recall.

"My name is Frank Moody, spelled M-o-o-d-y. I'm a manager for a manufacturing company in New Jersey."

Let's spell his last name: M-o-o-d-y. His first name is? Frank. Moody means gloomy, sullen, but Frank is smiling and cheerful right now. Since he has no lines in his face, we can presume he is usually friendly and cheerful. So let's remember his name by simply saying Frank Moody is not. Or, more to the point, Frank is not moody.

Now let's see how many first and last names you can remember. Got a pencil or pen and paper handy? I'll give you a slight hint for each person, and see if you can write down both the first and last names.

Our first example was a gentleman who has a bald pate. What's his name?

Number two was the lady in the hammock. Try to recall the two things she's doing and you'll have a clue to each of her names.

Number three is the skipper who's bringing in his boat.

Next is the lady meeting us at the door of a mansion. She's dressed in an outfit we usually associate with a man.

Still another lady. This one is in court awaiting her trial. She's got some money in her hand and is arguing.

One more to go, right? A cheerful chap. To be *Frank* with you, his happy face belies his name.

How did you do? Did you get six first names and six last names? Let's see if they're the right ones. In the order we met our guests, their names are Ralph Raitt, Katie Lyback, Louis Dockswell, Colleen Butler, Gloria Betancourt, and Frank Moody.

Did you get them all? It takes a lot of practice to learn to make up pictures for the many names you hear each day. Some are difficult, but practice eventually takes the work out of it. And you'll soon find that even foreign names are easier to understand and easier to spell. In fact, by the time we're through, you'll be able to remember what you want to remember for life.

Now let's see how you do on your own with a few names. Let's try a few more, and this time you think up a picture and an association for each name without my help.

Concentrate on a picture for the last name. Then try to tie the first name in with the picture. Remember, the more ludicrous and exaggerated it is, the better you'll remember the name. After you've invented a picture for each of these names, we'll go over our visual associations and see how mine compare with yours.

What sort of picture will help you recall the name, Bill Goodwine? He's manager in an audiovisual department. Bill Goodwine. G-o-o-d-w-i-n-e.

Number two. A lovely young lady from Canada named Jan Janssen. That's Jan for the first name. The last name is Janssen. J-a-n-s-s-e-n. How can you picture her name?

Number three. Bob Falzon. That's F-a-l-z-o-n, Bob "falls-on." Bob's a consultant.

Number four. A Spanish name. Carmen Padin. A pretty brunette, just five feet tall, Carmen Padin, pronounced Pah-deán.

There you have four names. Are you getting possible associations for them? Some pretty ridiculous pictures? Are you remembering to get lots of action into them? Don't forget to put yourself in the picture, even if just as an onlooker. Please! Don't censor yourself! Quickly make use of the first idea that comes to you. Picture it and hang onto it. You can improve on your associations later when there's plenty of time. Your first impression is usually good enough.

When you've collected some ideas, read right on and see what pictures I used to recall the same names.

For Bill Goodwine, I picture him drinking good wine. He offers me some. He's saying it's delicious. He's sniffing his glass, taking in the aroma of the wine. Picture that. And he tells me it cost a twenty-dollar bill. The picture tells me it's good wine. The bill helps me recall his first name, and that's it—Bill Goodwine.

The second name was Jan Janssen. She's a model and actress. I think of Sen-Sen, the breath sweetner, and the Jan-Jan stands out. I simply say to myself, as I picture her putting Sen-Sen in her mouth, "Jan Janssen, not Sen-Sen." The picture, the slight rhyme, and the repetition all make it easy for me to remember *Jan Jan*ssen. Not Jan *Sen-Sen*.

Bob Falzon was the third name. Bob falls on his face. I see him *bob* right up and brush himself off. Picturing his face full of dust or mud might make it even easier for me to recall the mishap. From now on, "falls-on" and "bobs up" should bring back his name whenever I see him. Again, the words we use should be as similar to the name as possible for accurate recall.

Now a Spanish name, Carmen Padin. Every time I hear the name Carmen, I see the star of the opera with a rose in her mouth. So I just reverse it. Every time I see the picture of the rose in the young lady's mouth, I recall that the first name is Carmen. The last name Padin is more difficult. Remember, it's pronounced Pah-dean (in Spanish, *a* is pronounced *ah* and *i* is pronounced *ee*). Well, then, I picture Carmen taking the rose from her mouth and giving it to her *pa,* who is the *dean* of a college, and he's dressed in robes that convey the picture. Think of the phrase "Carmen's pa is the dean."

Keep working on visualizing ridiculous scenes as you

31

meet new people. Make rhymes, invent visuals based on action or appearance. The more you work at it, the easier and the more fun it becomes. And the better your memory, the more confident you'll become. Again, practice is the best instructor. And remember, it's going to be a lot easier to make associations and remember names when you're actually face to face with the people whose names you'll want to learn.

Just for the fun of it, and to show you how all sorts of name-associations can work, here's a list of names from A to Z, with possible associations. Can you think of even better associations than mine? (By the way, see if you bump into anyone you know on the list.)

Names, Names, Names—from A to Z

Ray Angel: Picture him with wings and a halo, and even a ray of light shining from his body.

Louise Barrington: Louise's Bar is giving rings away by the ton. Picture her in a wedding gown.

Dale Caddy: A dale is a valley. Picture Dale caddying for Jack Nicklaus and winning a Cadillac ("caddy") for being the winning caddy. They're in a dale trying to get the ball over the hill, and singing "Over hill, over dale!"

Frank Decker: He's pounding with a Black & Decker hammer, tenderizing frankfurters.

Diane Emerson: Diane is Emer's daughter, not Emer's son. And she's eating Steak Diane.

Dave Fairman: See him as a judge. He's a fair man in his rulings. Picture him as King David with a crown on his head.

Ann Garber: She's waving a baton, leading the Jan Garber Band, but now it's called the Ann Garber band. And they're playing a medley from *Annie Get Your Gun*.

Jack Hackathorn: He's swinging a jackhammer instead of an ax, trying to hack a thorn off a tree.

Patricia Irish: She's wearing a dress of shamrocks and you're giving her a pat on the back on St. Patrick's Day.

Bruce Judd: Try a rhyme: Bruce Judd is not a dud, even though he's covered with mud.

Barbara Kraft: Eating Kraft Cheese like a barbarian. A bar of cheese, of course.

Mike Lewis: Picture him at a microphone (a "mike") shaking hands with comedian Jerry Lewis and laughing at his jokes.

33

Don McDonald: He's singing "Old McDonald had a farm, and on this farm he had a Don."

Oliver North: Pretend he lives on Oliver Avenue North.

Carol Orr: See her rowing a boat with two Oars (for the two r's in her name) and singing a Christmas Carol.

Rita Platt: She's wearing platinum rings, one on each of her ten fingers, and is singing "Rio Rita!"

Tim Quinn: Again, a rhyme. Maybe "Tim Quinn has a double chin," or "Tim Quinn drinks double gins." Or "Tim Quinn has to win."

Nancy Rutledge: See her walking high up on the ledge of a building, stepping carefully along in the rut of the ledge. You can be calling, "Nancy, be careful!"

Emmett Sanders: He's eating Kentucky Fried Chicken, and shaking hands with Colonel Sanders, the founder. You're a Cockney saying, " 'E met Colonel Sanders."

Mary Tagliaferri: It's pronounced Tag-lee-a-ferry. So she's putting a parking tag on a ferry boat named Robert E. Lee. She's not merry about having to tag a ferry boat named Lee.

Morris Underwood: Morr-is under wood typing on an Underwood typewriter.

Jane Van Hercke: It's pronounced her-key. So Jane is trying to open a van with her key. From the window of the van a man is saying: "Me Tarzan; you Jane!"

Arthur Welch: He's drinking Welch Grape Juice and when he's finished he says: "Ar-thur any more bottles left?"

John Xavier: See him as St. Francis Xavier with a cross, blessing the crowds of people. And St. John is beside him doing the same thing. John and Xavier.

George Yellen: Hear George Yellen, "Help! I've been robbed!"

Bob Zink: He's bobbing for a zinc ball instead of a popcorn ball.

35

4
How to Remember Lists

PICTURE–RHYME ASSOCIATIONS

Next, a solution to a second major need of people today: how to remember a list of things. Lists plague us constantly. Yours may be a shopping list, ideas you don't have time to write down, or jobs you've got to do, or even laws and regulations you have to cope with. Everything we've taught you so far will serve you well here.

Although many of the principles we've learned for remembering names also apply to lists and rules, we need still another system to improve our recall in this category.

What I'm going to teach you now is a third system, a basic system you can use for the rest of your life. The difference between the last system and this one is that the devices you use here never change. You use them for every situation, like a Morse code. The things you will memorize with this method are usually temporary—you certainly don't want to remember your shopping list forever!—but they'll stick in your mind just as long as you want to retain them.

Two reminders: While you can use the devices I suggest, recall will be far more successful if you dream up your own. And second, my promise still holds—if you improve your memory in any one classification, you'll improve it for everything. So let's sharpen your recall of *lists*.

Put on your thinking cap and let's get to work. I want you to read this list out loud so you can learn it faster. Remember, because this is your permanent code, you want to be able to call on it quickly whenever you need it. So drill it into your head.

We're going to use rhyme-words for the numbers one to ten. We have to learn these by heart before we move on, so run down the list, out loud, ten times, going faster and faster. Make it a loud, rhythmic chant (never mind who's listening; they'll be envying you later on!)

One, **Bun**
Two, **Glue**
Three, **Key**
Four, **Store**
Five, **Drive**

Six, **Mix**
Seven, **Oven**
Eight, **Bait**
Nine, **Dine**
Ten, **Hen**

Once again, repeat the whole thing, but *faster*. Now try them backwards because you've got to know this list by heart backwards, forward, even inside out. The entire system depends on knowing this code as well as you know your own name.

So let's go through it again, *backwards,* then work on them individually.

What's number two?
Number three is?
What's number seven?
And number ten?
What's the number for store?
Number five is?
And number three is?
What is number nine?
The number for hen is?
Number eight is?

Once again now, let's go through the list forward, then backwards. Start with one, head to ten, and then go back to one.

For good measure, one more time, but this time backwards first and then forward. And give it pace and rhythm. From ten back to one, and then from one to ten.

Alright, that's fine. The closer you associate these

39

numbers with their rhyme-words, the better you'll remember any association later.

Now—how do we use these rhyme-numbers? Easy!

Starting with number one, what's the rhyme? **Bun.** Picture yourself about to take a bite out of a hamburger. What
you bite into is the *number one item on your list*. You picture item number one tucked like a hamburger into the
bun, and you're biting into it—item, bun, and all. Add
ketchup, pickles, onions, lettuce. Make it colorful, make it
ridiculous. The more action, color, and exaggeration you
visualize, the easier remembering becomes.

Right now just fix in your mind the picture you'll be
using for one: **bun.** You are taking a bite of a big hamburger and as you bite into it, you discover that instead of
biting an all-beef patty, you're biting the *first object you
want to remember*. There'll always be an object—even if
what you want to remember is abstract, you'll translate it
into a concrete object to tuck into that hamburger bun.
We'll discuss the choice of objects once we learn the picture-rhyme associations.

Number two is what? **Glue.** For two, glue, picture yourself pouring glue from a giant jar all over the *second object
you want to* remember. Build in action, add a good deal of
the ridiculous, even the bizarre. See yourself getting stuck
in the glue as you're pouring it all over the *second object
you want to remember*.

Number three is what? **Key.** You have a key in your
hand and you unlock the door to a closet in your home.
You open the door and out pour hundreds of the *third object you want to remember*, they chase you, they're bounc-

ing all around you, you're buried under the *third object you want to remember*.

Let's review. What's the rhyme-word, and what's the picture, for number two? **Glue.** Pouring glue over the *second object you want to remember* and getting stuck in it yourself with glue all over everything.

What's the permanent picture for number one?

Eating a big hamburger and finding inside the **bun,** not beef, but the *first object you want to remember*.

And what's the rhyme-word, what's the picture association, for number three?

Key. Opening a closet door in your home and staggering back as hundreds of object number three come pouring out.

Next, number four. And the rhyme-word for four is? **Store.**

Picture yourself going into your favorite grocery store. When you get inside, you see that the store is stocked with only one item, thousands of them lining the shelves, and stacked in piles over every inch of the floor. You can't believe that there are so many of that one item. And that item is the *fourth object you want to remember*. You see a sign that says "Free today." You grab a cart and start filling it with that fourth object. You're grabbing so many so fast that they're spilling all over the place. That's the picture for four, **store.**

Number five is what? **Drive.** You're driving a car down the street. Suddenly you put on the brakes because you see a giant thing in the road. The thing you see is the *fifth object you want to remember*. You can't stop, so you slam

41

right into it, and it shatters into a million pieces. Little bits come flying down all around you, and some hit you.

The rhyme-word for number six is? **Mix.** You're in your kitchen with a mixing bowl. You have a spoon in your hand. You are mixing away in the bowl when you realize that what you're stirring is a whole bunch of the *sixth object you want to remember*. They're multiplying fast. They're pouring out over the top of the bowl! You try to catch them so they don't fall off the table. Some do fall, and they break as they hit the floor.

Let's review again. What's the rhyme-word, and the picture, for number two?

Glue. You're pouring glue all over the *second object you want to remember,* and as you do, you're getting glue all over yourself, so that you're stuck to object number two and can't get away.

And the picture and the rhyme-word for number four?

Store. You're in the grocery store and you find it's packed with the *fourth object you want to remember*. That's all there is in that store, just object number four by the thousands. And they're free today, so you start loading up a cart, and you're spilling the stacks all over the place.

What's the rhyme and what's the picture for number one?

Bun, hamburger. You're eating it, but when you start to eat it, you bite into the *first object you want to remember* instead of beef.

What's the rhyme and what's the picture for number three?

Key. You're opening your closet at home, and out come hundreds of the *third object you want to remember*.

Number six rhyme-word and picture are what?

Mix. You've got a mixing bowl and you're stirring a whole load of the *sixth object you want to remember*, and they're being stirred right out of the bowl and falling on the floor.

Now the rhyme-word and picture for number five?

Drive. You're in a car, you're driving. You put on the brakes, but you still slam into the *fifth object you want to remember*. It gets smashed into hundreds of pieces that come falling down all around you.

Here's a new one, number seven. What's the rhyme-word? **Oven.** Picture yourself opening your oven. Inside, you find object number seven, burning. There are a dozen of them—you pull them out. They're hot and smoky.

I realize that learning these permanent rhyme-words and pictures is a little like going back to school. But that's just it! It's so easy once you understand the method. After you've made these associations your own, once you know them by heart, there's nothing to it. These pictures never change—unless, of course, you find better rhymes and pictures than mine. But whatever choices you make, once you do choose, the numbers and letters will remain the same. Learning those ten will work wonders. You'll see what I mean shortly. For now, just keep concentrating and absorbing the ideas I suggest.

All ready for number eight. Rhyme-word for eight is? **Bait.** You're at the lake, fishing. On the hook at the end of

43

your line is object number eight—the bait! Suddenly he picks something up and throws it at you.

Number nine is **dine.** This is fun. You're at your favorite restaurant, ready to eat. Dinner is served. But on your plate, instead of steak, what do you see? The *ninth object you want to remember.* You stick your fork in it, you slice it with your knife, you even put ketchup on it.

Rhyme-word for number ten is? **Hen.** Picture a big hen. Instead of laying an egg, the hen lays the *tenth object you want to remember.*

And there you have ten rhyme-words and ten pictures. Let's see if you can remember them. Try the first five, quickly.

One, **bun.** A hamburger, *object number one* in the bun instead of beef.

Two, **glue.** You pour glue over *object number two* and you get stuck to it.

Three, **key.** You're opening a closet and out pour hundreds of *object number three,* practically burying you.

Four, **store.** Your favorite store is filled with nothing but *object number four.* They fall all around you and even into your cart. You tumble into a cart filled with them.

Keep going! Try to master at least five.

Five, **drive** You're driving a car, and you slam into *object number five,* which shatters.

Six, **mix.** You're mixing a whole mess of *object number six;* it pours out of the bowl.

Seven, **oven.** You're in your kitchen and a dozen of *object number seven* are burning in your oven when you open it.

Eight, **bait.** You're fishing at a nearby lake and your bait is *object number eight.*

Nine, **dine.** You're in your favorite restaurant dining on the *ninth object* you want to remember. You take your knife and fork and dig in.

Ten, **hen.** A big hen has just laid—not an egg, but *object number ten.*

You must have noticed by now how quickly visualizing, repeating, and associating can produce recall of these permanent numbers, and how much the rhyme-words and pictures help. Once we start picturing the actual objects, it will be even easier. Remember, *you* must be in the picture. Visualize *yourself* involved in the action. Build in as much exaggeration as possible. Make it ridiculous, absurd, crazy. Make it colorful, bright, nutty. *Make it exciting.*

You've learned ten basic picture associations for remembering any list, such as rules, facts, or ideas. The numbers and rhyme-words will be important as well when it comes to remembering other things—names and jokes for example. But right now, let's see how well you can do recalling a list of ten difficult items. I will teach you how to take difficult abstract material and remember it automatically. I want you to learn how to form objects—concrete images—from nebulous, abstract concepts. Some of the objects we're going to work with now will seem strange, or weird, or silly to you, but I assure you there's a practical value to what we do next. Also, I want you to learn something worthwhile the first time we actually put the picture-rhyme technique to use. We will be simplifying

(continued on page 48)

45

Picture-Rhyme Associations

You'll always picture the object you want to recall if you keep in mind these associations. These rhyming number-and-word combinations are *permanent*. So are the associations, the mental images. Only the objects you want to recall will change.

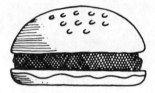

ONE, BUN, hamburger bun—but instead of a beef patty in the bun it's the first object you want to recall. You bite into it.

TWO, GLUE. You'll be pouring glue on the second object you want to recall, getting stuck to both bottle and object.

THREE, KEY. As you unlock a closet in your house, dozens of the third object you want to recall come tumbling down on you.

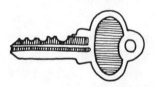

FOUR, STORE. Visualize yourself going into your local supermarket. All you see in the store is the fourth object you want to recall—stacks of it piled high on all the shelves and on the floor all around.

FIVE, DRIVE. You're driving your car. You see something big ahead, the fifth object you want to recall, but you can't stop. You smash into the object, breaking it to pieces.

SIX, MIX. You are mixing something in a bowl. It's the sixth object you want to recall. You're mixing lots of it—stirring so hard that it's all falling out.

SEVEN, OVEN. You open an oven and find a dozen of object number seven burning. You take them out of the oven.

EIGHT, BAIT. You are fishing at a nearby lake. You use object number eight as the bait on the hook.

NINE, DINE. You're in your favorite restaurant, waiting for the dinner you've ordered. The waiter arrives from the kitchen and puts a platter down in front of you. You're about to dig in when you realize it's not a steak but the ninth object you want to remember.

TEN, HEN. A big hen. Instead of laying an egg, she lays object number ten.

important abstract material, but I won't reveal what you've learned until you've mastered it. People rarely forget these first objects, not even years later.

The Mystery List: See How Well You Do

Believe me, this is a beauty. Learning to recall a shopping list will be child's play after this exercise. Here we go! Concentrate hard on putting the objects I mention into the rhyme-picture we've established for each of the numbers one to ten. It's your responsibility to imagine yourself in action, to put some color, some absurdity into your mental association.

The object we want to remember for number one, **bun,** is a *statue* of a strange-looking man. A big statue. Picture it in the bun. Take a bite! Chip a tooth! Got it? You are the one in the picture holding the bun and biting in and reacting. Build in an "Ouch," or a "Whaaaat?"

Number two, **glue.** Don't backtrack! Never mind the mental review. Keep up with me. The number two object we want to remember is a *tapestry*. It's huge and it's red, white, and blue, with the words *God Bless Us* woven into it in giant letters.

Get a vivid impression of each object. Visualize yourself in action with the object just as we taught you in learning the association. You should be all sticky now from number two, **glue;** you should be stuck hands and feet to the tapestry, and you ought to be seeing your own frustration, hear yourself saying, "God help us," or maybe "God bless us."

Number three, **key.** Picture hundreds of *posters* falling

48

out of the closet as you turn the key and open it. Some pictures the word *Saturday* plus a star. Others show the word *Sunday* and a cross. You're buried in posters. Actually manage to see yourself with the key, opening the closet, and being buried beneath tons of posters. It'll be the weekend before they dig you out.

Number four, **store.** The object to remember this time is a plastic *mold of a parent*. Picture thousands of them in the store, piled everywhere. Some read: World's Greatest Father! Others read: World's Best Mother! Every face is bright, colorful, and smiling, and the molds come in all sizes. And they're free, so you start filling your cart. Don't worry about the piles spilling all around, just jam molds into that cart. And even visualize yourself falling in among them.

Let's review. Answer out loud if you can.

What's falling out of the closet? *Posters.* What's on the posters? Saturday, with a star, and Sunday plus a cross.

What's the object for number one? The statue of a strange-looking man.

What's stuck in the glue along with you? *Tapestry.* What words are on it? God Bless You.

What's number four? Plastic molds of mothers and fathers, the World's Best mothers and fathers.

What's number three? Posters reading Saturday or Sunday, with a cross for Sunday, a star for Saturday.

What number goes with the statue of the strange-looking man? One.

Hang on to those and let's add some more objects.

For number five, **drive,** picture *an old lady.* You're

driving, going too fast, you can't stop. And—yes, I'm sorry—you hit her hard. Visualize yourself jumping out and getting into action. She's unconscious. You hope she's still alive.

Let's move on now and concentrate only on the next object for number six, **mix.** Put a *tree* in the picture. See a sign hanging on each branch, and each sign reads *adult*. A tree for adults, perhaps. Picture a lot of small *trees,* all with signs on their branches. That's what you're mixing in the bowl. You're the chief stirrer for a lot of trees.

Next is number seven, **oven.** The object? A *box* marked *"stolen jewelry."* Visualize a lot of boxes all filled, all marked, all burning in the oven. Picture a dozen *boxes* marked *stolen jewelry.*

Number eight, **bait,** is next. The object is a *metal picture frame.* Visualize a metal picture frame as the bait on your line to catch fish. See a *metal picture frame* as your bait.

Let's do another brief review.

What's in the oven, burning? *Boxes* of *stolen jewelry.*

What are you mixing in number six? *Trees,* with branches labeled *adult.*

Whom do you hit while driving? *An old lady.*

What's number one? The *statue* of a strange man.

What's in the closet in three? *Posters* reading *Saturday* or *Sunday,* with a *star* and a *cross,* respectively.

Which number is the *tapestry* with *God Bless Us* on it? Two.

What's the bait on your hook? A *metal picture frame.*

What's number four? Plastic statuettes of *mother and father* labeled *World's Best.*

Two more to picture. For number nine, **dine,** we visualize a book, *The Merry Wives of Windsor.* Picture a nice fat volume on your dinner plate. You're trying to dig into it with a knife and fork.

Number ten, **hen.** You want to remember a *TV set* with the name *Jim Nabors* on it. Jim Nabors' name on a big *TV screen,* right over his picture. Visualize his picture on the TV screen.

There you have ten objects for ten picture-rhymes. Now, see if you can remember all of them. Try mentally, silently, to identify the objects we've pictured. Start with number *one, bun,* and identify just the object that goes with the number. Write them all down if it's easier.

Try them backwards now from ten to one. Start with number ten and identify each number and object down to one.

Now, let's see how we do taking them out of order. Try to answer each question.

What's number five?

What number is the tapestry that reads *God Bless Us?*

What's number seven?

What number is the *TV set,* the one where the hen lays the object with "Jim Nabors" in it?

What's number nine?

What number is the *statue* of the *strange man?*

What's number four?

What number is the *poster* reading *Saturday* or *Sunday,* the one that shows the star or cross?

What's number six?

I've asked you for only nine of the ten. Can you tell me which one is left?

51

A *picture frame*. It's the *bait* on the hook. It's number eight.

You remember I told you that these ten objects have a practical value. True; they'll help you remember something important for the rest of your life. The objects you've pictured in these mental associations represent the *Ten Commandments of the Old Testament*.* You've just learned to make objects, concrete pictures, out of a series of abstract laws, the *Ten Commandments*.

What was the object for number one? Yes. The *statue* of the *strange man* reminds us of Commandment number one: *I am the Lord, thy God, thou shalt not have strange Gods before me*.

The object of number two was what? Yes, and the *tapestry* with *God Bless Us* on it signifies Commandment number two: *Thou shalt not take the name of the Lord thy God in vain*.

What was object number three? *Posters* that said *Saturday* plus a *star,* or *Sunday* with a *cross*. Commandment number three: *Remember thou keep holy the Sabbath day*. What was object number four? *Plastic molds: mothers* and *fathers*. Right! And Commandment number four is quickly and accurately recalled: *Honor thy Father and thy Mother*.

Surprised at how easy it is? And you can probably dream up more satisfying objects and pictures than the ones I've suggested. Also, you can use other rhyme-words and pictures for the numbers once you've mastered the ideas. Gun and sun also rhyme with one. And for two, there's shoe, zoo, crew. I happen to prefer glue because it suggests absurd associations so readily.

*Roman Catholic version.

Here's how the last five work. The number five object was what? Right, an *elderly lady* is hit by your car. And the fifth Commandment is: *Thou shalt not kill*. I hate being bloodthirsty, but the picture should be strong and vivid and wild enough to bring back the object quickly. And the object reminds us in this instance of the Fifth Commandment. Do you remember the picture for five? Drive is used for whatever object we want to recall.

Next, the object for number six. What was it? An *adult tree*. Got the pun? Commandment number six is: *Thou shalt not commit adultery.*

And the object for number seven? *Boxes* marked: *Stolen Jewelry*. Probably being returned to the owner. But the Commandment we want to recall is: *Thou shalt not steal*. You can even tuck a policeman into the picture along with the boxes, and have him putting handcuffs on you right in your home; that ought to give you a more vivid image.

The object for number eight was what? *Frames*. And what does it mean to *frame* a person? It means to lie about him. In other words, a frame-up.

And that recalls for us Commandment number eight: *Thou shalt not bear false witness against thy neighbor.*

The object for number nine was what? The play, *The Merry Wives of Windsor*. Commandment number nine should pop into mind: *Thou shalt not covet thy neighbor's wife.*

And object number ten was the *TV set* with the name *Jim Nabors*. Commandment number ten should be easy: *Thou shalt not covet thy neighbor's goods*. Including his *color TV set!*

53

Congratulations! You now know the *picture-rhyme association system,* and you've learned to recall easily ten objects. And you've tackled the toughest stuff first, really abstract material. From now on it's *got* to be easier.

And now that you understand the system, you'll need lots of practice. What should delight you is that you won't need to write down everything you want to remember any more. Just use the one-through-ten *picture-rhyme method,* and you'll be able to rattle off a list of ideas, or things to do, rules, laws, names, jokes, points for a speech or a meeting—anything. The system is marvelously versatile. Simply make an object out of what you want to remember, and picture it with one of the rhyme-numbers. You don't have to worry about overworking your pictures; you'll forget the shopping lists or to-do lists fast enough once the activity's behind you, and the picture-rhymes will be fresh and clean and ready for the next use.

I usually use the *picture-rhyme association* technique for the points of a speech, for shorter lists, rules, laws, and principles. You can also use the method for recalling names, although visualizing alone should be sufficient. (Remember Bill Goodwine? And the bottle of wine marked *good,* with the dollar bill taped to it?) All you need to stamp his name indelibly on your mind is to use a rhyme-word such as *bun* for *one.* Put the bottle of wine in the bun. And there you are!

I had two objectives in writing this book: first, to make remembering easy for you; and second, to help you learn the systems just by reading and practicing. You can find dozens of books and magazine articles on memory, many of them with techniques, systems, and devices that are strikingly similar. And yet thousands have read them without improving their memories. The problem is that these masters of memory rarely tell you exactly *how to do* what they want you to do. I want you to have the how-to's. But more importantly, I want to make you practice, practice, practice. Not tomorrow, but right now, as you work with me. Recitation is the hammer that's going to drive this material into your memory.

So we're going to practice some more. I want you to find out just how easy and practical the basic, permanent number, rhyme-word, and picture technique is. So here we go.

For one, **bun,** think of a number one name in hamburger service—McDonald's, or Burger King. *One, bun, hamburger bun,* should be quick and easy to recall.

Number two, **glue.** Tell yourself that number two is a sticky one to recall. "Sticky" will remind you of *glue.*

Number three, **key.** Picture a key ring with *three keys.* Any one of them fits the closet you open.

For number four, **store,** picture a *four*-story grocery store. Four stories—*four, store.*

For number five, **drive,** think of a car with *five*-wheel drive. Crazy, but *crazy* is just what produces a better memory. Picture a sporty car with a manual shift, a car that has lots of drive.

Six is **mix** and you can think *six mixes.* Number *six, six mixes.*

Seven, **oven.** Recall Hansel and Gretel pushing the witch into the oven. *Seven, oven.*

Eight, **bait.** Picture the object as the bait on your fishing line.

Nine, **dine.** *"Nine* to *dine"* is a fine idea for a picture! And *"dine* at *nine"* in the evening will help cement the number to the rhyme-word.

Ten, **hen.** A hen lays the object, not an egg.

Later on we'll illustrate many ways you can use this picture-rhyme method, but now I'll show you how well the technique works when you want to remember ideas that pop up suddenly and you don't have the time or the inclination to write them down.

While working on this book, a number of obligations piled up on me. Since I was concentrating on writing about memory, I simply used the number-rhyme technique to file the demands away for quick recall later. I didn't have to interrupt my work as the thoughts nudged me. I merely associated them.

First, I had to send a check for $30 to the dentist. So I pictured for one, a bun, holding a set of false teeth chomping three ten-dollar bills.

Next, I had to remind myself to send a letter to a company in Palm Springs, California, setting the dates for a fall training course. So for two, I pictured myself stuck with glue to a small palm tree while I sang "September Song."

The third thing I had to do was to arrange for one of my associates to represent me in Atlanta. So for three, key, I pictured an airplane. When I opened that closet, all kinds of model planes fell on me. The associate's name is Falzon (there really is a Falzon), so the picture was easy for me. I just said to myself, "As I stand there opening the door, the airplane *falls on* me."

Next, I had to get some brochures together for a Ms. Turner at a client's training department. I simply used four, store, and there was Ms. Turner, hundreds of Ms. Turners everywhere in the grocery store, including the chcek-out counters. Ms. Turner was everywhere I turned.

Finally, I had to see that arrangements were made for a course to be held at a hotel in Dallas. The chief chore was to order videotape recording and playback equipment. I simply used five, drive, and the object I smacked into was a *giant TV set*. I mean a TV as big as all Texas!

I'm happy to report that before two days had passed, I had not only recalled all five of those tasks—I had accomplished them! I just wanted you to see how easy and practical the picture-rhyme association method is for instant mental storage of all sorts of information and ideas.

By now, it should be easy for you to remember a shopping list for the grocery store, the hardware, drug, or department store. You've got the system. All you have to do is picture the object and incorporate it into one of the one-to-ten rhyme-pictures. If you wanted to shop for milk, a head of lettuce, ice cream, a prescription, birthday cards, a door lock, and paint, what would you do? Simply put one item at a time into the pictures. Visualize the bottle of milk in the bun. See the head of lettuce covered with glue and stuck to you.

So that's the picture-rhyme association method. But— remember the thirteen original colonies? Right! You can also stack the items. And that's what we'll go into now.

First, I want you to notice that I listed three grocery items, two drugstore, and two hardware items. Organizing them into related groups always makes remembering easier. Learn to do it automatically whenever you face a list. It's particularly important for the technique we're going to study next.

THE STACK-AND-LINK METHOD

Our memories can play tricks on us. Still, you've learned some tricks of your own to control it, haven't you? Well, now you're going to learn how to use my fourth basic technique. You've already met this technique— remember the thirteen original colonies? Once you've mastered the *stack-and-link technique* to recall longer lists, you'll have two major techniques and you can lean on the one that works best for you. As time goes on, you'll discover that both are effective. I did; I use them daily.

Here's the basic idea: Whatever you want to remember—a poem, a speech, a batch of sales ideas, or a shopping list—can be stacked and linked mentally. It's another way to recall things quickly, but it's also the tool you'll use when you want to memorize something permanently. I prefer the *stack-and-link* method when I'm trying to memorize a series of more than ten items, whether it's a list of jokes, items, rules, or those thirteen colonies. I recommend it, too, for remembering textbook material, whether for a summary or a test. You can also use the stack-and-link method to recall names in a special order, perhaps chronologically. Start with the name symbolized by an object, such as the wine for Goodwine. Then *link* each successive object symbolizing a name. Remember, though: stack-and-link's greatest benefit comes from the fact that the items on your list are linked in sequence and can be recalled consecutively, whereas in the picture-rhyme association method, items must be recalled one at a time.

As an exercise, take out a sheet of paper and see how many of the original thirteen colonies you can recall. Start with the delicate chinaware. . . .

How did you do? If you didn't get all thirteen this second time around, go back to chapter one and practice some more. And take my word for it, the method works like magic once you get the hang of it and start using it regularly.

Let's look at some of the practical benefits of stack-and-link. You're bound to find yourself in the following list.

Stack-and-Link for the Salesperson

If you're a salesperson, stack-and-link can be enormously useful. People buy *benefits,* and as a sales representative, you need to know thoroughly the *benefits* to your prospect of your product or service (I find most salespeople don't.) Stack-and-link is a quick, easy way to learn them.

I'm going to ask you to visualize a number of objects along with me, and then we'll go over the method once more from your point of view.

First, picture a safe, an office safe three feet high and two feet wide, fitted with a combination lock. Second, visualize the name on the safe, in huge print across the door: TOTAL, T-O-T-A-L, Total Safe Company. There is an *ax* jammed into the crack of the door with the handle sticking out. There's a *card* attached to the handle of the ax; you see on it the word *special*. There's a a *woman* holding the handle of the ax. She's *dressed in black*. Hanging on to the black dress of this woman are *two children,* a little *girl* and a little *boy*. The little girl has her hair done up in *curlers*. The little boy is holding a *balloon* with the word *free* on it. A *man* comes up to the boy and pulls the balloon down as *he says: "lower."*

The nine ideas stacked and linked in that scene represent the *benefits* available to customers who allow a banker or insurance man to handle their estate planning. Here's what the objects represent: First, a *safe* is a place where you *save* things. The benefit of an estate plan is that it can *save* thousands of dollars. The name *Total* on the safe means you'll benefit from *total* estate planning—that is, by having one counselor handle all cash, property, insurance, bonds, investments, and so on. Next, the *ax* suggests that this counselor can cut or *eliminate taxes* and can cut costs through a comprehensive plan. The card on the *ax* marked *special* means that *specialists*—professionals—will be managing your investments. The *woman in black* is the widow who will be given the *power of attorney* through the plan. The *two children* remind you that a *trust* is provided for survivors. The little girl's *curlers,* the sign of a *permanent* wave, signify *permanent financial security* for the surviving children. And the *balloon* with the word *free* on it reminds us that the property passes *tax-free* to the children. The *man* telling the boy to keep the balloon

60

lower indicates the benefit of *lower taxes* on future settlements, such as might arise on the death of the mother.

There are nine actual, specific, meaningful benefits stacked and linked in that picture, nine ways in which estate planning that includes a trust can save people thousands of dollars. I have found that most salespeople don't really know the benefits of their product—or couldn't reel them off on demand. The stacking technique makes it so easy. Just trust your creativity, humor, and experience to provide you quickly with ideas for objects to picture, and then build your associations one on top of the other.

Stack-and-Link for the List Maker

You've learned one way to remember a shopping list. Let's try the stack-and-link method on the same list we used for the picture-rhyme technique. Remember what you were buying? Milk, lettuce, ice cream, and some drug and hardware items. Let's picture the *milk* first. Visualize a giant tub of milk. Make it enormous: Exaggerate! Floating in the tub of *milk* is a huge head of *lettuce*. It's covered with chocolate *ice cream*. The ice cream is still quite hard, and there's a bottle of *cough syrup* sticking out of it. The label tells you clearly that it's cough syrup. Tied to the neck of the bottle is a big *birthday card*, one of those huge one-dollar cards; this one reads "Happy Birthday!" Fixed into the top of the card is a *door lock*. If you pull up on the lock, it will drag with it the whole string of items dangling from the card: the bottle of *cough syrup*, the *ice cream*, the *lettuce*, and that giant *tub of milk*. Next, tipping over on

61

top of the lock is a *can of white paint*. It's dribbling down over the lock, over the card, the cough syrup, the ice cream, and the rest.

All that should be easy for you to recall, even though the list was just for fun. Once you have your own real-life list, personal obligation will make you work even harder at concentrating, visualizing, and inventing memorable associations. In fact, a little practice will make it so easy, you'll wonder why they didn't teach this whole thing in school. It's a good question. And there's a better one: Why don't they give memory courses in our schools *now,* so people can learn more, learn faster, and learn more easily? Fortunately, there's an international emphasis on memory today, and a trend is setting in that will eventually make memory courses a regular part of the school curriculum.

Stack-and-Link for the Speech Maker

I've been making speeches all my life—since grade school, in fact, early in World War II. I used to go to PTA and church groups to sell U.S. Savings Bonds, then known as War Bonds. I'd give a ten-minute inspirational speech about Uncle Sam's need for money. In those days I didn't know any better—I memorized my speech the hard way, word for word.

Once I grew up, I discovered how unnecessary it was to memorize speeches. And how dull it was for the audience, because spontaneity was totally lacking. So I began a new system—I used an outline of key words and phrases, and pretty soon I was winning speech contests, while my audiences grew bigger and more receptive.

A few years later, I found an even easier way to remember: I started using the two systems I've just taught you, and I found both of them excellent. I know a lot of top speakers and teachers for whom the stack-and-link system works well, but I favor the picture-rhyme method. I still use a written speech outline on occasion, just as I occasionally use a written outline for teaching. Most of the time, however, I use the picture-rhyme method to provide myself with a mentally organized outline of key words or ideas.

I used to give a talk on human relations that I called "Tools of Leadership." I could do a well-rounded job in two minutes, or I could expound on the subject for an hour. And I assure you, I could stand up before an audience right now and talk for an hour on that subject or on a host of others, because the associations I've made for my many speeches are unforgettable. Even today, I teach all day and often all week using these memory techniques.

Here's how I recall the quotation to open the talk on leadership. For number *one,* I picture a can of coffee tucked inside the *bun.* That reminds me of the opening of the talk, a quotation by the late John D. Rockefeller, Sr., who once said, "The ability to deal with people is as purchasable as coffee or sugar; and I'll pay more for that ability than any other quality on earth." Once I've established that my subject is human relations, I go on to number *two, glue.* A mental picture of page *70* of the *Reader's Digest,*

63

covered with glue and stuck to my hand, reminds me of a survey in that magazine that revealed that 70 percent of people fired from their jobs were fired for one reason: their inability to get along with their fellow employees.

In a talk I often give on public speaking, I picture for number one a set of chattering false teeth with lots of silver in them. That reminds me of the quotation by the silver-tongued orator, William Jennings Bryan, who said, "The ability to speak effectively is an acquirement, not a gift." Nice point. The same can be said about a dependable memory—it's an acquirement, not a gift.

To motivate a group in a classroom or audience for a speech on time management, I picture for number *one, bun,* a big clock with the name Drucker on it. In a split second I've got a handle on a quotation by management expert Peter Drucker: "The number one requirement for effectiveness as an executive is to know where your time goes."

Do you see how simple it is? For every major point of any talk I give, or any classroom lecture on any subject, I use objects I've fitted into the picture-rhyme association method or the stacking method. They not only work; they work wonders!

Stack-and-Link for the Chairman of the Meeting

Whenever you conduct a meeting, a conference, or a discussion, you will of course have a written agenda. Everyone at the meeting should have a copy. In fact, it's good practice to see that each person has the agenda a day or so ahead of time. But there will be times when you'll want to get away from the written agenda. For those times, just make objects out of the points you want to discuss. Then use the stack-and-link method—or, if you prefer, the picture-rhyme association method—to bring your points leaping to mind.

Let's say you want to ask your department heads to give oral reports on what they're doing to curb cigarette smoking in restricted areas. Simply visualize a neon sign showing a cigarette; visualize a giant red X drawn over the cigarette. To stack and link, picture the sign down on the floor as object number 1. If the second item is to get all department heads to complete vacation schedules for their people, just picture a fishing rod with a big fish on the line. Visualize the fishing rod connected to the sign, and a big fish jumping at the end of the line. You can put all the points of the meeting in that one linked stack, whether you have five or fifteen ideas to discuss.

In fact, if there are more than ten ideas to remember, you should always use the stacking method. It's usually the best for a long list, particularly when the items have to be recalled in order—and quickly.

So far we've learned a verbal trick (rhyming) and three visual tricks (mental pictures, picture-rhyme, and stack-and-link.) Now comes another verbal trick. I call it TATA.

TATA: TAKE ADVANTAGE OF THE ACRONYMS

An acronym is a word made up of the first letters of several other words. It's a kind of verbal shorthand. UNESCO, for instance, is an easy handle for the somewhat unwieldy United Nations Educational, Scientific and Cultural Organization. RADAR comes from Radio Detection and Ranging. AWOL stands for Absent Without Official Leave.

You can use this device as I do. As a learner, I use acronyms to classify and highlight the essence of what I'm learning. As a teacher or lecturer, I use them to recall outlines for lessons, talks, or meetings. One acronym I use in the classroom is ALPO, which you know as a dog food, but which I've borrowed without shame. In *my* ALPO, the A stands for Assess students' needs, the L is for Listen to students' wants, the P for Plan for participation, and the O for Objectives of the course. It takes about five minutes to make up a reminder for all the essentials without burying yourself in notes.

In a talk on the subject and also in a cassette series on listening I did for AMACOM, I used the key word itself, LISTEN: L for Look at the other person, I for Identify the evidence; S for Speak only in turn; T for Think of what the speaker is saying, the essence of the message or conversation, E for Emotions—check them; And N for Never interrupt. That one word, the acronym LISTEN, is my whole outline, or at least my master word for the talk. I can also break the same talk into two parts, the basic and the advanced principles of improved listening. I use the acronym LADDER for the six basics: Look at the person; Ask questions; Don't change the subject: Don't interrupt; Emotions—check them; and Responsively listen. And the acronym AIM (let's aim to be a better listener!) provides three finer points: Anticipate the point a speaker is making;

Identify the evidence; Mentally summarize the essence of the talk.

The better you can organize what you want to recall, the easier it is to recall it. And that's the value of the acronym—it can help you organize even general information. For instance, if you ask me my hobbies or interests, I think immediately of PHD, MD, YW, PS. The letters stand for Photography, Humor, Drama; Music, Dancing; Youth Work; and Public Speaking. Recall is quick as a wink.

One professor I know has an interesting acronym on the subject of management: He uses the word BOSS to outline some of the responsibilities that attach to that job—B is for Be in charge; O is for Observe company rules; S is for Standards that should be kept; the second S is for Strive for excellence. And remember: an acronym like this can also serve as the structure for a speech.

All the techniques and methods suggested in this book fall under the heading of *mnemonics*. It's a big word, and I've avoided using it till I had shown you what it means, instead of just telling you. Mnemonics is a system of principles or formulas designed to assist or improve your memory. And now that you've learned these methods, you know more about memory than most speakers and teachers. The fact is that a vast number of speakers, preachers, and teachers are tied to notes on a lectern; they read practically everything they have to say. Try introducing those *you* know to the techniques you've just learned—you'll make life easier for them. In fact, spread the good word everywhere, to children especially—you'll make listening and *learning* more fun for everyone! What's more, teaching others is one of the best ways of teaching yourself. You'll be surprised at how useful the practice can be!

One last word: to understand everything we do from now on, you really should ground yourself thoroughly in the techniques we've studied so far. These are your ABC's!

5
The Art of Remembering Numbers

NOW WE'RE GOING to tackle the toughest challenge of all: numbers. In this world of ours, everything is recorded by number. The child must remember his address; grandpa has to remember his social security number. We all have to remember telephone numbers by the dozens, and dates, and zip codes, and statistics, and prices, and the last figure in our check books. How do we do it?

There are several systems for recalling numbers, but frankly I think you'll find them baffling and confusing— harder to remember than the numbers themselves. Since this book is dedicated to memory made easy, I'm going to suggest some methods that are technical but not complex. Also, I'll be including a few simple but helpful techniques that work with certain classes of numbers.

Again, organization is the key to this kind of memory work. And the best way to organize is to maintain a compact booklet or set of index cards, some system where you can fit numbers by some appropriate classification. Nothing replaces written record keeping when it comes to numbers, dates, and statistics. I use three-by-five and four-by-five cards all the time. I buy five hundred at a time (I'm one of the biggest purchasers I know of file cards!), and I've always got a pocketful with me. I write down everything: numbers, names, ideas, dates, statistics. When I get back home or to the office, I transfer the data to a file system. I keep files on everything.

Nothing helps memory so much as writing it down. You can see it, you can review it, and it's there on file in case you forget it. Some kinds of information are too important to risk leaving to memory. Losing a name or a phone number can mean losing business and income, losing a friend, maybe even losing a profitable idea.

So get in the habit of keeping information in written form. I keep the names and phone numbers of everyone I've met in the last twenty years on index cards, and I've added notes on each card so I can remember the person the name attaches to. Not even a memory expert could possibly remember every name, every number, every idea, every fact for years without that kind of help.

In addition, my files include data on diet, current news,

movies, guarantees, health, coupons, even one on the White House. I have an idea folder. I have folders on every management topic, including time management, motivation, communication, and on and on. If you save it, you can use it. If you don't save it, if you don't file it, you find yourself having to trust to libraries. But why should you have to? Instead of borrowing their material, borrow their systems. After all, libraries have the best file systems, the best cross-file systems—in short, the best organization possible. Take a lesson from them: Organized notes and files support your memory, and make it trustworthy. And they're far more dependable for vital data such as numbers, figures, statistics, and dates.

Now let's look at some memory methods you can use when you want to be independent of your files, when you want to *mentally* store and recall numbers of any kind.

THE NUMBER–ALPHABET SYSTEM

Over the years and even centuries, man has devised techniques of various kinds to recall numbers. Perhaps the most enduring and popular of all these systems is the method of substituting letters of the alphabet for the numbers zero to nine—or more commonly, one through nine and then zero. The ten letters we'll be using represent the ten basic consonants of the English phonetic alphabet. It will pay you to memorize this system as soon as possible, because it will make a big difference in your day-to-day efficiency.

The letter for number 1 is **t.** They are similar in appearance: **t,** like the number 1, has just one downstroke.

Number 2 we associate with **n**: note that **n** has two down-strokes. Number 3 is **m**, which has three downstrokes. Number 4 is represented by **r**, the final letter and sound in the word four. The substitute letter for number 5 is **l**. Hold your hand up—the five fingers with the thumb extended form a capital L. Number 6 is represented by the letter **j**, which almost looks like a 6 reversed, as it would be in a mirror. Number 7 is always paired with the letter **k**; 7 comes after 6 just as k comes after j. Number 8 is matched with **f**. When you write a script f, with two loops, it looks like an 8. Number 9 is represented by **p**, and p is virtually a 9 when you visualize it backward, mirror-fashion. Zero, the last, is a **z**, obviously because zero includes the last letter of the alphabet.

If you find it easier to remember a word than a single letter, just relate the phonetic alphabet to parts of the body. I've found this method the easiest of all. 1, **t**, is toe; 2, **n**, is nose; 3, **m**, is mouth; 4, **r**, is rib; 5, **l**, is leg; 6, **j**, is jaw; 7, **k**, is kidney; 8, **f**, is foot; 9, **p**, is palm, but it's also **b**, as we'll discover, so think of a Pat on the Back. 10 is **s** as well as **z**, so think of s for stomach.

There you have the phonetic sounds of our consonants. Since we don't use the vowels, they're available to us to help turn numbers into words—a nice trick to help us remember a sequence. For example, let's assume that an important telephone number is 432-2345. Substituting our alphabet code, we get the consonants **rmn nmrl**. We now use the vowels a, e, i, o, and u to form words. Immediately, I see I can make the two words *roman numeral*. When I need to remember that phone number, it's simple to drop out the vowels and translate the consonants **rmn nmrl** to the number 432-2345.

Practice what you've learned so far. There are some code charts coming up to help you. Again, 1 is **t**, 2 is **n**, 3 is **m**, 4 is **r**, 5 is **l**, 6 is **j**, 7 is **k**, 8 is **f**, 9 is **b** or **p**, zero is **s** or **z**. Learn to know them as well as you know your own name. Practice them backward, forward, and inside out. Only when you know them instinctively can they help you. And they will, any time and every time numbers are important to you.

Let's look at a few possible uses for our number-alphabet.

Use It to Remember Your Social Security Number

Let's take a make-believe Social Security number—say, 584-21-2158. The first step is to substitute the consonant code, which is **lfr-nt-ntlf**. Now combine the consonants, in that sequence, with vowels to form words. The result can be absolutely senseless—remember, it's easier to recall the absurd or ridiculous. The words that come to mind are *a life run to a U.N. tealeaf*, but they might have been *loafer, not nutloaf*. Once you have latched on to your phrase, all you need do to decode it is drop the vowels.

Use It to Remember Your Credit Card Number

Try this system on your credit card numbers, or that endless driver's license number. The trick here is to break the longer numbers into groupings of three or four digits each. In fact, that's a rule of thumb for remembering anything. Group things. Break them up into more manageable forms. Your credit card number may already be stamped in groups on your card; use those groups. If not, break it up yourself. Let's try a make-believe number: 4211 153 314 913. Thirteen digits, arranged in four groups or clusters. Now take a pencil and paper and write down the number-alphabet for that set of numbers. If you need to, go back a page or two to review something. Next, add vowels to create words with some sort of meaning, however nonsensical.

For the four grouping of numbers we've chosen, I came up with this crazy sentence: *Run it total mom, to rip Tom.* Drop the vowels and you have the substitute letters for the credit card number. I admit it's a nutty combination of words, but remembering it is a lot easier and much more trustworthy than trying to remember the numbers alone. You probably created a much more sensible sentence. Fine! Just don't be *too* sensible!

For zip codes or area codes, the idea is the same. I use the word *notion* for the New York City area code. Drop the three vowels and you have **ntn.** Translated, that's 212.

And that's just a start. There's more to the alphabet number system. Altogether, it takes a good deal of work to master it and then a lot of practice to make it work well for you. But once you do, it's an excellent—and simple—system, even when we add the remaining consonant sounds to the ten basic consonant phonetic sounds I've already taught you.

For number 1, **t,** we add **d** and **th.** For 6, **j,** we add the consonant sounds **dg** (as in wedge), **tch** (as in latch), **ch, sh,** and **soft g** as in gender. For 7, **k,** we add **hard c** as in

74

cat, **hard g** as in dog, **ng,** and **q.** For 8, **f,** we add **v** and **ph.** For 9, **p,** we've already added **b.** And for zero, **z,** we've added *s,* and we'll also add soft *c* as in city.

Since this is a system of phonetic—not spelled—sounds, we can consider double consonants as one. For instance, *baseball* becomes 9095 once you drop the vowels. The first **b** is number 9. The **s** is zero. Another **b** for another 9, and the **l's,** both of them, become 5.

You've probably noticed that we don't use *h, w,* or *y,* because they are half vowels. And the *x* is out, because it's represented by two sounds. Let's take the word *mix.* The **m** is 3; **x** as **ks** would be 7 for **k,** zero for **s.** So the word *mix* translates to the numbers 370. *Remember, it's the phonetic sound that counts!* In *xylophone,* where *x* sounds like *z,* we'd use it for zero. *Xylophone* would thus be 0582.

A few more rules. Silent letters, such as the *k* in knit, knock, or knob, are disregarded. So the word *knit* would transpose to 21. In words such as *bring* and *thing,* the *ng* sound translates to 7, as do the *q* and the *ck* in *quick* and *quack. Bring* and *thing* translate to 947 and 17. *Quick* and *quack* equal 77 each.

Use It to Remember Any Long Number

Even a long list of numbers such as this one is easy: 9501103574502940. Just transpose it to consonants and add vowels to form a sentence. *Please date small girls in pairs.* Drop the vowels, decode, and you've got your number again. Remember that double consonants, like the *l* in *small,* count as one, since only one *l* is actually pronounced.

Here's a complete visual summary of the alphabet-number system. First, because the why's are as important as the how's in helping you remember, I give you the rationale, the logical explanation for each substitution. Then I've added a handy chart for you to refer to until you learn the code. Study it! Memorize it! Then, once you've got the system down pat, experiment and discover for yourself how versatile it is.

Remembering Numbers by the Alphabet System

1 is **t**	Both have one downstroke.
2 is **n**	There two downstrokes in **n** to remind you it's number 2.
3 is **m**	Three downstrokes make **m** number 3.
4 is **r**	The word four has an **r** in it as well as 4 letters.
5 is **l**	Hold your left hand up with the thumb out sideways. Your 5 fingers form a capital **l**.
6 is **j**	You can picture **j** as a 6 reversed, as in a mirror.
7 is **k**	7 comes after 6; **k** comes after **j**. Since 6 is **j**, 7 is **k**.
8 is **f**	In script, **f** is often written with two loops, so it looks like an 8.
9 is **p**	**p** is virtually a 9 when you see it backwards, as in a mirror.
0 is **z**	**z** is the last letter of the alphabet, and zero starts with a **z**.

On the next page, you'll see the complete English phonetic consonant alphabet in handy chart form.

It may help you to relate the consonant alphabet to parts of the body. I've found this technique to be the most reliable for fast learning and even faster recall.

1 is **t,** so think of teeth
2 is **n,** so think of nose
3 is **m,** so think of mouth
4 is **r,** for rib
5 is **l,** for leg
6 is **j,** for jaw
7 is **k,** for kidney
8 is **f,** for foot
9 is **p,** for palm; 9 is also **b,** so think of a pat on the back
0 is **z,** but 0 is also **s,** so think of stomach

One sentence can be used as an acronym to recall all the key consonants:

The new moon rose late in June; kiss Fred pretty soon!

Complete Number-Alphabet Table

1	2	3	4	5	6	7	8	9	0
t	n	m	r	l	j	k	f	p	z
d					ch	ng	v	b	s
th					sh	q	ph		soft c
					tch	hard c			
					dg	hard g			
					soft g				

STACK-AND-LINK NUMBERS

The technique you learned earlier can also be applied to numbers. Simply remember to break up any long list of digits into clusters of two, three, or four each. Translate the clusters into words that can be pictured, and stack and link the pictures as we did the thirteen colonies.

Let's try to stack some numbers. 4891147432. First step: break the list into smaller clusters. I like to break it into two's. For 48—**r** and **f**—we can spell roof. For 91—**p** and **t**—how about pot? For 14, tree. For 74, car. And for 32, we can spell man. So we have roof, pot, tree, car, and man. (Notice how important it is to use a concrete word if you want to find a picture for it.)

Now we can stack and link. Picture the roof of a house with a pot on it, a really huge pot. Growing out of the pot is a gigantic tree as tall as the Empire State Building. Hanging from the limbs of the giant tree are red cars that look like drooping red flowers. And on top of the tree, standing in a red car, is a tall man who's waving at us. See how easy it is? You've reduced a string of digits to words; you've stacked the objects the words suggest. When you're ready to recall the numbers, bring the words back to mind, starting with roof. Drop the vowels, translate, and you've got the digits.

ALL THOSE STATISTICS!

Statistics are much easier to recall than most people believe. Let's take a few examples. There are 17,500 restaurants in New York City. Do you feel an urgent need to remember that fact? Then use this idea. Even if you ate in a different restaurant in New York City every morning, noon and night, it would take you 16½ years to eat in all of them. Remember that statement and it should be reasonably easy to compute the total.

The FBI in Washington processes 21,000 fingerprints a day. Using the number-alphabet you learned earlier, 21,000 translates to **ntzzz.** Add a *u* and you've spelled *nutzzz,* three **z**'s; you just picture thousands of nuts falling into your hands from a peanut plant, while you carefully put your fingerprints on each one of them. To translate, take *nutzzz,* drop the vowel, and translate the letters to 21,000.

Another way to make statistics easy to remember is to break them down so that they have meaning. Here are some actual statistics broken down into meaningful—and, in fact, startling—form. In the United States, there's a murder every 27 minutes; a robbery every 82 seconds; an auto theft every 34 seconds; a case of aggravated assault every 76 seconds; a theft of more than $50 every 7 seconds; and a rape every 10 minutes. Experts say nine out of ten rapes are not reported, so that would mean there's a rape committed every minute. You can recall these smaller, more memorable statistics by using your number-alphabet. Use the conversion chart if you haven't yet got it all down pat. Then do a little back-and-forth between words and numbers. For instance: rape, **r** and **p**, gives us 49. Now try the trick in reverse: Change the *statistic,* 60 (seconds) to the letters **sh** and **s,** and form a word—let's make it *shoes.* Picture 49 shoes, and there you have the statistic and the category all in one-easy-to-remember phrase.

AND ALL THOSE DATES!

Did you ever think of associating a date in your life with a historical date? For example, Charles Lindbergh made his historic solo airplane flight across the Atlantic in 1927. That's the year I was born, so it's easy for *me* to remember Lindbergh's feat. But you're not me, and you may have been born in some less splendid year. You can still remember 1927—just use the number-alphabet. 1927 becomes **tpnk,** in which you could choose the two words *top nike*. Nike, of course, is the guided missile. Picture it flying over Lindbergh's airplane. To recapture the date, drop the vowels from *top nike,* translate, and there you have 1927.

You should find it quite easy to recall any date by using the number-alphabet. Let's say you want to remember a date in 1927, such as August 23rd. Start by converting August to the number 8, which is the eighth month; write that with 23 and you have 823, or **fnm.** Transpose this to the two words *fine aim* and add that to *top nike*. To recall August 23, 1927, simply drop the vowels from *fine aim, top nike,* then translate, and you've got the date instantly.

AND ALL THOSE PHONE NUMBERS

Here's another simple technique that sometimes works with telephone numbers. Check the dial to see if you can make up a single word or two words out of the letters that are combined with the numbers on the dial. If you can get a sensible word from the dial letters, you'll have no trouble recalling the numerals accurately and instantly. For example, in Chicago, if you dial CARPETS, you get a large retail outlet selling carpets. In Houston, if you dial WANT ADS, you get a local newspaper advertising department. In Minneapolis, dial RAW BEEF and you get a midtown liquor store. This store advertises by skywriting the phrase "Dial RAW BEEF." Once you've seen that against a blue sky, you aren't apt to forget it.

LET'S REVIEW A FEW THINGS

There's no easier way to remember numbers than to use our alphabet-number system. But whether you use that system or any of the others, you have to do your homework first. I'm repeating myself, you say? Sure I am, but it's vital. And after you do your homework—after you get the techniques down pat—you've got to use them. You've got to concentrate, think, rhyme, visualize, and associate. You've got to practice the memory fundamentals constantly. The more you use the systems, the more quickly remembering will become second nature for you. I can assure you that using the number-alphabet system especially gets easier with practice.

Another reminder: Improving your memory in just one area—names, for instance—will improve it for just about everything. And the key to that improvement is organization. This means setting things in order, arranging them systematically. Just as peace comes from order in the world, peace of mind stems from order in our minds. Writing things down prints them clearly on our minds and

81

helps us to file information in an orderly system. But of course, writing things down is only one technique. We can't always carry our files with us. The point is to be able to *remember,* to be able to drag a fact out of our heads when we need it. And for this, organization is absolutely essential. So remember what I say: Organize your materials! It will make it easier for you to use any one of our memory systems.

There are several ways to improve your facility with the phonetic alphabet. Play Scrabble—the crossword game—or Anagrams, a word game that is an ancestor of Scrabble. Do crossword puzzles. Keep a dictionary at hand while you read, and look up any mysterious words. And when you write, look up fresh new usages in a thesaurus of synonyms and antonyms. Any and all of these tricks will help increase your vocabulary. And the more words you know, the more words you can create with your number-alphabet, and the more rhymes, the more acronyms, the more pictures you can come up with.

6
Special Challenges
to Your Memory

WE HAVE FOND MEMORIES and feelings, agreeable thoughts, and ideas we want to *remember*. Many events and experiences stay with us for all our lives because of their impact on us. If I mention kindergarten, what comes to mind? Probably some happy thoughts which will stay with you no matter how old you get. I can recall my teacher's name. I can remember making a bookcase, taking naps on a rug, and seeing movies.

This one example illustrates how well the mind works and how superbly it organizes and classifies our experiences and memories. This fact only underlines the idea I've been stressing throughout this book: There's a great deal we can do to improve our memories if only we took the trouble to organize our thinking. For many of us, memorizing (or learning by rote) is the only way we can remember things. But memorizing is the hard way to do it, and it's not always dependable.

Is there a better way? In fact, that are several—and they all start with *organization*.

"I CAN NEVER REMEMBER JOKES"

Most people need help recalling jokes. Every week I hear someone say, "I just can't remember jokes," or "I can remember jokes but I keep forgetting the punch lines." Joke telling is an art, and part of that art is hanging on to the details—*including* the punch line. (Except, of course, for the occasional joke or pun that's so bad we'd like to forget it entirely.)

Well, how *do* we remember a joke? If it's a short one, memorizing it word for word is easy. But for anything longer than a few sentences, memorizing takes away the spontaneity, and makes the delivery too stiff, too formal. You face the same danger when you try to memorize a speech, a poem you have to recite, or the material for a test.

And what happens if you lose your place while you're making a speech, or draw a blank while you're taking a test? It could be a disaster, especially if you're in front of an audience: You become embarrassed, and so do your listeners. And even if you manage to get through your memorized material, you may lose the freshness of delivery so important in putting across your point. You've watched speakers working from memory. There's a faraway look in their eyes, a faraway sound to their voices. Only professional actors who've studied the material for months can manage to work from rote. And even then, they will usually do a little relaxed ad-libbing just to bring life to the characters they're playing.

If you study the pattern of the top stand-up comics, you'll discover two things: First, they have an organized system for remembering their jokes, usually key words and categories; second, they keep the story brief and they tell it in their own words. You notice this most clearly when you've heard two or three comedians tell the same joke. Each uses the same punch line, but each gives the joke his own personal touch. They're spontaneous—and they're funny.

Henny Youngman is known as the king of the one-liners. Bob Hope and Milton Berle specialize in brevity. Alan King, Danny Thomas, and Myron Cohen go in for the longer anecdote, but none of their material is ever as long as the average story you hear at a party. Dragging out a joke, loading it down with excessive detail, is a sure way to kill it.

Organization is an essential key for recalling jokes. Concentrating when you first hear the joke will help you understand it. Repeating it will help you learn it. Writing it down and reviewing it will help. Telling it, of course, is often the best way to learn it. But to assure recall, do what Henny Youngman does. *Henny tells his jokes by category.*

"I've got five brothers-in-law. The first brother-in-law is a genius: he opened a tall man's shop in Tokyo. The second brother-in-law says he's a diamond cutter—he mows the lawn at Yankee Stadium." I can do the rest of them just from having heard him describe the five brothers-in-law over the years. It's one of his key categories.

So, the first rule is: *Organize by categories:* wife or husband jokes, political jokes, movie jokes, ethnic jokes, sports jokes, mother-in-law jokes, outer space jokes, teacher jokes, or cab driver jokes. Or you can break a given category down even further. Under the category of sports, for example, you can tell baseball jokes, or football jokes, or tennis jokes. Most comedians, professional speakers, and teachers remember jokes, speeches, and stories by using subject categories.

Another important rule is to *pick key words* you can picture (using the systems we discussed earlier) or you can simply develop the ability to remember the joke by recalling that key word.

Henny Youngman can go on and on without notes for an hour. By now—and he's in his seventies—he'd be lost without two key techniques: categories and key words. But even he sometimes forgets a joke. When that happens, he says, "I forgot the joke!"—and he always gets a big laugh because he's shown he's human. This is a good model to follow. If you ever find yourself in the middle of a joke and you suddenly can't recall how it ends; admit you forgot it!

I recently watched Henny do a show in Chicago. He was rattling off one-liners in machine-gun style, when he stopped, having apparently lost his train of thought—he probably couldn't think of a category he hadn't covered: (By that time he'd been on stage for half an hour.) What he did was to start chatting with the people seated around the stage. "How are you? Where are you from?" he asked. And he happened to say to one group, "Are you comfortable?" But before they could answer, you could see that he was back on the track. The word *comfortable* had reminded him of a joke. It was the key word to his punch line. The joke is about a little old Jewish man who was hit by a car. The policeman puts a blanket around him, and sits him against a wall to wait for the ambulance. The patrolman asks, "Are you comfortable?" And the man says, "I make a decent living. . . ."

The ability to recall a joke by classification and by the use of one or two key words comes through practice (as does the art of telling a joke or a story clearly and concisely). Arranging jokes by categories is easy; picking a key word is more challenging, but with a little practice you can get the hang of it. Or, instead of focusing on one key word, why not concentrate on the most important words of all—the punch line? Tell a top comedian a punch line and he'll tell you the whole joke. Try it yourself. If you learn the punch line, you'll usually remember the details. Just be sure to stick with the short anecdotes. Brevity may be the soul of wit, but it's also the soul of clarity.

Let's try this technique on a couple of jokes. Write down or mentally select a key word or two to recall the idea, paying particular attention to the punch line.

Two women are talking. The first says: "I understand

your husband drowned and left you two million dollars. Can you imagine? Two million dollars—and he couldn't even read or write!''

The second woman answers: "Yes. And he couldn't swim, either.''

What would you choose as the key word to help you recall that joke? For me, it's "couldn't swim either," or "drowned," or "two million dollars." By the way, you could easily stack this joke, or put it into a rhyme-word association. You might picture a bag of money, a gigantic bag marked "two million dollars." Picture it at the bottom of a swimming pool and you have the essence of the joke.

Or how about this one? A fellow asks a girl's father for permission to marry his daughter. The father asks, "Can you support a family?" The fellow answers, "Yes, I can." And the father says, "Good, there are seven of us!"

What would you use as a key word or words? For me, "marriage" is the category, "support" and "seven" are the two words that help me recall the joke. For stacking, you can picture the fellow on his knees asking the father's permission. You can add the seven members of the girl's family, standing around them in a circle, expectantly. Or use the rhyme-word association. Either technique—the key words or the picture—should make it easy to remember the joke.

It should be even easier to recall one- and two-line gags. Talking about his wife, a man says, "She missed her nap today—she slept right through it!" Picture a woman curled up on a sofa, sleeping. Classify it under wife, sleep, or nap.

Let's go over the basic points in recalling jokes. First, keep them short. Second, write them down. Third, classify them by categories. Fourth, use key words to recall the joke and the punch line. Fifth, practice them on friends, or dictate them into a tape recorder.

Children can be marvelous audiences to practice on. They can even teach us lessons about telling jokes—and remembering them. Some children's television programs entertain kids while teaching them how to remember things. PBS's *Sesame Street,* for example, uses all the techniques we've been talking about. Kids who watch the program learn their letters and numbers by seeing them on the screen—and seeing is one of the easiest ways to learn. Second, the show uses constant repetition. Third, it uses comparison and contrast with things that are similar and dissimilar.

Watch *Sesame Street* yourself some day—you may learn a lesson on how to remember. Watch the stars of the program—especially the puppets—use memory methods just for fun. Recently, the characters went through two charades on memory. In the first, a boy named Johnny was sent out to buy a loaf of bread for his mother. He kept repeating, "Loaf of bread, loaf of bread." Then he met a neighbor, a little girl who said, "Look at my new doll!" And he went away saying, "New doll, new doll!" Next, he saw his friend Bill, who said, "Come to the baseball game!" And Johnny proceeded to the store saying, "Baseball game!" The last thing he heard before he reached the store was a fire engine. You've probably guessed the punch line: When he finally got to the store, Johnny said to the grocer, "One fire engine!" Johnny's mind had wandered. Every passing experience pulled at him. This shows that concentration and association are more essential than repetition when you want to recall a detail accurately.

The second sharp memory stunt on *Sesame Street* involved the famous Cookie Monster. Someone asked him why he had a cookie on the table in front of him. To remind him of a circle, he replied. Why did he want to recall a circle? The circle made him think of a square, and the square helped him remember a checkerboard, which made him think of games. Games, he continued, remind him of football. Football made him think of music, which reminded him of bells. Bells reminded him of an alarm clock. And the alarm clock told him it was time to eat his cookie.

Unless I'm wrong, the only objective of this "Shaggy Cookie" story was to entertain the children and their parents. Or was there a hidden message beneath all the fun? This was also a lesson in the importance of visualizing, repeating, and associating to remember. I can assure you it works; after all, I remembered those two stories simply because the actors practiced the laws of memory discussed in this book.

"A POEM LOVELY AS A TREE"

There's nothing lovely about having to memorize a poem. The rote system is still popular, but it's very difficult unless you remember the on-off rule: Study a while, then leave it alone for a while. When you have to memorize or study, you can learn more at a faster rate if you work for a half hour or an hour, *then* take a break.

Poetry that you don't want to recall word for word can easily be paraphrased if you use the key-word technique. Remember Joyce Kilmer's "Trees"?

I think that I shall never see
A poem lovely as a tree.

There are two *I's* in the couplet, plus the words *think, see, poem,* and *tree*. You can picture a brain for *think*. Two *eyes* can remind you both of the letter *I* and the word *see*. *Poe* in *poem* can stand for Edgar Allan *Poe* and his *poetic mind*. And a *tree* is easy to picture. For me, the picture of a *brain* with two eyes on the branch of a tree would be a fine clue. For a longer poem, I'd use the stacking method—I'd link pictures of the key words from successive couplets. The surprising thing about this method is that you can usually remember even a long poem *word for word* much faster and much more securely than by rote memorization!

Let's turn to a more difficult poet—Shakespeare. How would you recall the dagger scene from *Macbeth?* Macbeth recites these lines on his way to kill King Duncan: "Is this a dagger which I see before me?" To remember the quote, picture a man with a dagger above his head. The second line continues, "The handle toward my hand." Picture the handle pointing down. "Come, let me clutch thee." Picture Macbeth, a crown on his head, clutching at the imagined dagger. He goes on, "I have thee not, and yet I see thee still." Picture Macbeth looking at his empty hands, or picture just a hand in the air, palm up, and maybe a giant question mark over it. Did I say more difficult? Shakespeare's vivid imagery makes his verse much *easier* to remember than other poetry!

HOW TO LEARN TEXTBOOK MATERIAL

These days, there's a boom in adult education, and people of all ages are attending school. Evening and even weekend classes attract young and old alike. But when it comes time to take tests, the hard work begins. It becomes necessary to learn and remember facts, figures, dates, history, and general information. This section will help you handle these problems.

Few people in school—regardless of their level of education—have been exposed to as many memory aids as you have in this book. Most of them don't even know that it can be easy and fun to improve their memories; they are still learning by rote, by repetition, or by memorization.

Earlier, we learned how to use acronyms to remember material. Let's see how acronyms can help in school. You probably learned the names of the five Great Lakes with one of the most famous acronyms: The first letter of each of the lakes—Huron, Ontario, Michigan, Erie, and Superior—spells *HOMES*. You can use acronyms to retain many facts that you need to pass tests. As a matter of fact, acronyms are often good ways to recall information you need in business, or even socially.

In Minnesota, my home state, I learned an acronym that

made it a snap to remember the nicknames of athletic teams in the Big Ten Conference. I can still recall it thirty years later without ever having written it down: Big Gophers Can Be Supreme By Hitting In a Hard Way. The first B stands for the Badgers of Wisconsin; the G, and the word Gophers, for the Minnesota Gophers; the C for the Cats, the Wildcats of Northwestern; the second B for the Buckeyes of Ohio State. The S is for the Spartans of Michigan State, the third B is for the Boilermakers of Purdue, the H for the Hoosiers of Indiana, the I for the Illini of Illinois, the second H for the Hawkeyes of Iowa, and the W is for the Wolverines of Michigan. This one sentence has settled more arguments than you would believe. I never needed guesswork; I just used the acronym, *Big Gophers Can Be Supreme By Hitting In a Hard Way.*

Incidentally, you don't have to be a student to find acronyms helpful in school. I discovered this when I started teaching. A student named Ed Cavanaugh in one of my classes in New York gave a talk that consisted of all the acronyms I had used during a semester in a communications arts course. They included the 5-B formula—Be Brief, Baby, Be Brief—and the 5-P formula—Proper Preparation Prevents Poor Performance.

But you've learned some other ways to remember textbook material. You can use the number-alphabet for any and all dates, statistics, facts, formulas, and numbers. You can use the number-rhyme method for names and lists. And you can use the stacking method for facts and information of all kinds. Let's review these techniques and see how you can apply them to textbook learning.

Let's say you want to recall the fact that Mt. McKinley rises 29,141 feet into the sky. How would you remember a number like that? If you use our number-alphabet, you'll find that the numbers translate to *nptrt*. Now, add a few vowels, and you might come up with the phrase *an ape, a toe, or a tie*. When you need to recall this statistic, simply drop the vowels, and the consonants will translate easily to 29,141 feet. Notice that I used words that suggest climbing. It took me only a minute to think of these words—Apes climb; climbers stub toes; climbers *tie* a rope one to another—so the key words in the sentence—*ape, toe,* and *tie*—help remind me of climbing, and they also remind me that it's a mountain.

You can improve your recall of both poetry and numbers by concentrating, thinking, organizing, associating, clustering—in short, by studying the material. And by studying, I mean getting the complete sense of the communication, its logic, and its meaning. Take a few minutes to read over the material several times. Mark the key lines, the chief numbers or ideas, with a light-colored crayon: That always helps to highlight the essential data. And of course, organize it in categories, and choose key words.

Are you studying history? Or current events? You can use our methods of association for recalling important names. Almost everyone remembers that Machiavelli wrote *The Prince*. But few remember his first name—Niccolo. I try a rhyme-association: I picture him playing the piccolo. Picturing him wearing princely rich robes helps me recall the title of his book.

If your history textbook covers the period of the thirteen

94

colonies, then you're ahead of the game: You've already learned the names of the colonies. You've already learned what every religious book includes, too—the Ten Commandments. And you learned both of these abstract lists by the stack-and-link method. Use the same method to recall lists of events, personalities, rules, laws, and principles.

A WORD ABOUT MEMORIZING

If you can't depend on techniques of general recall, if you must memorize a poem or passage word for word, remember what I've often said: The art of retention is the art of attention. Analyze your material thoroughly. Think about the meanings of the words. One hour of intense concentration will accomplish more than years of dreaming. But take short—or even long—breaks every hour or so. Try to find associations for the new ideas you're learning. Pick out the key words or ideas, and mentally outline them.

These are the little tricks I've advised all along. But for memorizing, I'd add a few more: Memorize out loud; read the entire work; read it again; think of the meaning; read it again, and group the thoughts in your own words; read it again, and tell the thoughts in the author's words; work when you're at your best and your most alert. If you can space the job of memorizing over a few days or more, you'll learn it far more easily. Many speeches, by the way, can be learned thoroughly and then paraphrased. If you do that, you'll sound far more spontaneous and natural, and you'll avoid that glazed, frigid approach that comes from rote memorization.

95

7
Games for Practice and Fun

OUR LIBRARIES and bookstores are filled with books that tell you how to amaze your friends and neighbors. I've got a few simple exercises that I use for practice and for entertaining people.

For instance, I'm going to tell you how to memorize the pages of a magazine. But first, you have to learn how to remember a really long list of items—as many as you want to remember—using picture-rhyme associations. Then I'll demonstrate how you can combine the stack-and-link method with picture-rhyme associations to really learn enormous quantities of material quickly.

You've already learned rhyme-words for the numbers one to ten—*one, bun* down through *ten, hen.* To remember a much longer list, all you have to do is make one addition to your picture for numbers eleven through twenty.

For these next ten objects, use *one, bun* through *ten, hen,* but *picture the action taking place on the deck of an ocean liner.* If the eleventh object is a reminder to go to the jewelry store to get your watch, picture a big wristwatch ticking loudly inside the hamburger bun. But since you're eating the hamburger on the deck of an ocean liner out at sea, you know it's number eleven, not number one.

Here's the one change for items twenty-one through thirty. Use the same basic rhyme pictures *one, bun,* through *ten, hen,* but this time imagine all the action taking place inside an empty 747 jet plane.

For items thirty-one through forty, the action is at Yankee Stadium. The bun, the oven, the hen—all your basic rhyme-associations take place while you're standing on the field at Yankee Stadium.

I know this sounds crazy, but it works. It's new to you and you haven't tried it yet, so naturally you can't know how easy it is after only a few practice periods. You will rarely want to recall as many as twenty or thirty items, but you now know that you can do it. All you need is this simple extension of the picture-rhyme association technique.

For forty-one to fifty, you can picture everything taking place at Carnegie Hall. For fifty-one to sixty, you could visualize the associations and the action going on in a spaceship. Again, the more absurd the association, the more exaggerated the picture and action, the more easily you will remember!

If you feel this kind of visualizing is too far out or too difficult, stick with the stack-and-link method. Or make up your own rhyme-words for numbers eleven and up. For eleven, use the word zeppelin in the sky above you, and see the *object you want to remember* dangling on a wire from the airship, while you jump up and down trying to grab it. For twelve, use a word like valve; picture the valve pumping up and down with the *object* on top of it: You're either trying to hold the object on the valve, or you're trying to take it off. Visualize *yourself* as part of the action in the rhyme-word picture.

Try using the ocean liner, the jet plane, Yankee Stadium, Carnegie Hall, and the spaceship. They'll work effectively for you if you do the concentrating, thinking, and practicing necessary to master these techniques. Methods of this kind have served the experts and professionals reliably for years. And most of them got started for the same reason you did: because they had to remember things, but couldn't do it. They began by learning the basics and some of the finer points of memory, and went on to master the advanced techniques. Now *you* have the tools necessary to memorize a whole magazine in a quarter hour or less. You probably think that it's not possible—but it is, and I'll demonstrate how.

HOW TO MEMORIZE A MAGAZINE

To do this right, it's best to use a magazine with lots of pictures in it. Using the *Harvard Business Review* would defeat the purpose. Our goal at this point is entertainment, or just to practice our techniques, not to struggle with difficult material.

Using an old magazine, let's start with page one, opposite the inside cover. Page one shows an ad for Doral Cigarettes, in which a woman in a turtleneck is holding a lit cigarette. Using *one, bun,* picture a package of Doral Cigarettes in the bun, and have the model take a cigarette from the package as you bite into it. You now have the essentials for page one.

On page two is an ad for a cologne called *Charlie* showing a bottle of the cologne and a model in a pants suit, holding her hat and flashing a big smile. Revlon is the manufacturer. Using *two, glue,* imagine that you've tilted the bottle and you keep trying to shake some of the fragrance onto her wrist. But instead of cologne, out comes glue all over you, and all over the lady. See how easy it is? That's all there is to page two.

Page three is the easiest yet: the table of contents. Picture for *three, key,* a big table, a lot of big tables falling down on you as you open your closet at home. Along with the tables, photographs fall out—pictures of Joe Namath, Andy Warhol, and Dorothy Hamill (the skater who won an Olympic gold medal). That's the highlight of page three— the table of contents and the three personality photographs.

Page four has two key items. First, there's an ad for a Cross pen-and-pencil set. And the set is shown right next to the letters-to-the-editor column. Picture for *four, store,* sets of Cross pens and pencils all over the store, along with bags of mail stacked everywhere. You note that much of the mail contains sets of Cross pens and pencils.

Page five shows a huge bottle of Beefeater Dry Gin wrapped in cellophane. It's distilled in London, and on the label, there's a man carrying a spear and wearing the red uniform of the guard at Buckingham Palace. The gin is 94 proof. *Five,* of course, is *drive.* So picture yourself driving along and suddenly you see a giant bottle with the name Beefeater Gin in red letters. You try to stop, but you can't, and you smash into the bottle, plowing right into the red-uniformed guard on the label. Glass and gin are flying all over. You can taste the gin.

Pages six and seven of this magazine carry a double-spread ad for a camera. On the left, on page six, we see a color snapshot of a pretty model in a yellow broad-brimmed hat. She has long golden hair and a big smile. Behind this color snapshot, there's a Polaroid SX-70 camera. *Six* is *mix,* so you picture yourself mixing a lot of SX-70 cameras in a bowl, and they're popping out and falling to the floor. Picture the smiling model helping you mix, and helping you pick up the cameras.

Page seven, the right-hand half of the ad, shows a couple of color snapshots of the same smiling girl. One is a close-up of her face. The other shows her from the waist up with her arms folded. Below the snapshots, a man with a Polaroid camera is looking at you, as if he's about to snap your picture. Next to him, a pair of hands is closing a Polaroid pocket-size camera. Now, what's the picture-rhyme for *seven? Oven.* You look in your oven and you see a man as he tries to take a picture of you, as well as two snapshots of a smiling model.

What's in the bun? Doral cigarettes. What's number

101

two? Charlie Cologne. What's in the closet? Tables and pictures of Namath, Warhol, and Hamill. And what's in the store? Yes, sets of Cross pens and pencils, and tons of mail. The mail represents letters to the editor on page four. What's on page five? Beefeater Gin, a big bottle in cellophane. On page six, what are you mixing with the help of the model? Polaroid pocket-size cameras. And number seven, what's in the oven? A man taking your picture, plus color snapshots of a smiling model.

See how easy it is to visualize pictures for the pages of this magazine? All you need to memorize a whole magazine in a short time is the picture-rhyme association technique. We've just done pages one through seven; for pages eleven to twenty, remember the technique I explained earlier in this chapter. Picture all the action from eleven to twenty happening on an ocean liner; from twenty-one to thirty, on a 747 jet plane; from thirty-one to forty, at Yankee Stadium; from forty-one to fifty, at Carnegie Hall. From fifty-one to sixty, the action is pictured in a spaceship. From sixty-one to seventy, it's on a cloud; from seventy-one to eighty, it's on the beach at Waikiki; from eighty-one to ninety, it's in a blimp. Make up your own idea for ninety-one to one hundred. You need one hundred and twelve possibilities to cover every page of this magazine I'm using. Remember, you can *stack* the items from every few dozen pages. Linking them together and combining the stack-and-link and the picture-rhyme association methods works ideally.

This can be great fun on social occasions. I can assure you from years of experience that all you need do is have

102

someone at a party go out and bring back a magazine, preferably a new issue of *People* or *US,* and ask them to allow you ten minutes to memorize just ten to twenty pages. When you've used the rhyme associations, and then stacked and linked them, tear out the pages and distribute them to the members of the gathering. Then ask them to give you a page number, or mention an object from any page, and you'll give them the corresponding page number or object.

Test yourself right now on the issue we've been working with. If I say, "A bottle of Charlie Cologne by Revlon," what do you say? Quickly, "Page two!" if I ask you what's on page three, what do you answer? The table of contents and pictures of three stars: Joe Namath, Andy Warhol, and Dorothy Hamill.

After a while you'll not only amuse your friends but you'll astonish yourself. You'll be able to absorb and recall a whole magazine in a fifteen-minute period, and you'll do it expertly and accurately. The more you practice this exercise on an audience, even on one person, the sooner you'll be able to recall a whole issue.

There's one additional aid you can use when you have a magazine with more than one or two items or objects to remember on any one page. I always use the picture-rhyme technique for the major object on each page. Usually it's not too hard to add two or three other smaller items or pictures on the same page. But when there are more than two or three, you will always profit if you add the stack-and-link technique. Just stack the additional objects you want to recall on top of the first few.

We're still using our magazine. Page 8 has as its main picture a big *bowl* of almonds. The ad also contains a *can* marked Blue Diamond Almonds, and a small cellophane *package* of almonds. So for *eight,* with the rhyme word *bait,* you picture yourself fishing, and on your hook are a can, a package, and a bowl of almonds. That's the main feature of the page, and it's all you really need to convince people that your memory is exceptional.

But there are four other pictures on that page, and to amaze your audience even further—and maybe even amaze yourself—simply stack and link the remaining four objects to the bowl of Blue Diamond Almonds.

The first of the extra items is a huge *dessert glass* of *strawberries* covered wth *sliced almonds.* See the strawberries with the cream overflowing and pouring down onto the bowl of the whole almonds. The next object is an *open jar of candies* on top of the glass of strawberries. Visualize it sideways, so that some of the contents fall to the floor.

To review and continue, on top of the bowl of Blue Diamond Almonds for number *eight, bait,* we also have from page eight a big dessert glass of strawberries topped with sliced almonds. There's cream overflowing from the glass onto the bowl below. On top of the glass of strawberries, there's a giant jar of candies, prunes, and almonds. It's lying on its side atop the strawberries, and the candies are falling out. Now our next item is a slicing-board with fresh salad made with dark bread, Bibb lettuce, potato salad, and sliced onions topped with a dozen almonds. Picture the whole slicing-board balancing on the candy jar.

The salad is almost sliding off the board. The final item on page eight is a *cocktail glass* containing sherry. Picture that glass on top of the salad and tipping to one side, with some of the sherry overflowing onto the salad, the candies, and the strawberries, and dripping right into the bowl of almonds on the bottom.

There you have the complete story on page eight. Once you use the combined methods a few times, it takes just seconds to do what I've taken several paragraphs to explain. Your eyes take in the page instantly, and your mind goes to work automatically associating and stacking the objects for you. Remember to include action or motion, absurdity, *and yourself* in the picture. You can be sampling the almonds, strawberries, candies, salad, and sherry. Or you can picture yourself holding up the stack while it balances precariously and threatens to tip its contents all over you.

And that's it! The combined system of picture-rhyme and the stack-and-link method can help you to commit quickly to memory lots of items on the page of a magazine, the whole magazine itself, or even a long list. You'll find many other practical applications of this technique as well.

THE NAME GAME

Here's a game you can use for practice in remembering names. If you use it with a group of people who already know one another—say at a family gathering or at a club get-together—everyone should use assumed names. It works without any changes when you have a party of people who aren't acquainted: In that case, they'll use their real names.

First, get everyone seated in a circle or square and have them introduce themselves. They all have a minute to give both their first and last names and to describe their favorite hobbies, sports, or interests. Have them all say their names clearly, spell them, and give any special meanings the names might have. For example, I have a friend named Alberto Flores. (Flores, of course, means flowers.) In addition, people introducing themselves should, if possible, suggest ways in which others could remember their names. I know a speaker named Jim Larkey who talks a lot. Jim says you can recall his name by thinking, "Jim Larkey is full of malarkey." You remember I said you could recall my name, Robert Montgomery, by thinking of movie and TV star Robert Montgomery—think of him perhaps shaking your hand. Or you can think of Montgomery Ward, the department store.

The next step is for the second person to repeat the first person's name before introducing himself or herself. After he or she has finished, guest number three repeats the names of *both* the previous speakers before giving his or her own introduction. If you have twenty guests, the last person must tell the names, first and last, of all the nineteen members before introducing himself or herself. Then let all the others try remembering all twenty names. Each one should start with the nearest person and go right around the circle. To make it more challenging, ask each person to relate the hobby or favorite sport of the guest as well.

The name game can also work easily when you're in a group where everyone knows everyone else. Simply ask all the players to give their mothers' maiden names. The same rules apply. Pronounce the names, spell them, and suggest ways to remember them—mnemonic devices—if possible, including any meaning the names might have. For variety, each man can use his own middle name as a first name, teamed with his mother's maiden name. The women can use their own middle names with their mothers' maiden names. My name would be Leo Cyr. Leo the lion, of course, for my first name, and Cyr, C-y-r, for my last name. Cyr is French Canadian, and the sound, like S-e-a-r, makes me think of Sears-Roebuck, or maybe even Montgomery Sears instead of Montgomery Ward. In addition, sear means to burn, so you could picture me lighting a match and getting burned. Leo Cyr. It can be fun learning about people while mastering the art of remembering names. One caution: Use maiden names only when everyone knows everyone else. Always use people's real names when none of you are acquainted.

THE STRETCH-YOUR-MEMORY GAME

Since the art of retention is the art of attention, I'm including a guide-for-fun listening test. It's meant to increase your ability to concentrate and listen actively and constructively. Memory is dependent on listening and seeing, on keen observation and an alert ear.

107

Inform the group that you're going to tell them a brief story and then give them a test. You can use any story for the test, but I like this one, and I know it works.

"You are driving a bus down Main Street in your city. The bus has no passengers as it comes down the road. At the first stop, two people get on. At the next stop, three more people get on. At the following stop, one gets off. At the stop after that, two more get on; at the next, two get off; and at the last stop, one gets on." You can keep it up as long as you think it's practical. But for now let's check and see how well you listened.

First question: Who is driving the bus?
Second question: How many stops did the bus make?
Third question: How many people are still on the bus?
Fourth question: What street is the bus driver on?

Answer to the first question: You! I began by saying: *"You* are driving a bus down Main Street in your city." And there you have the correct answer to question four— *Main Street*. The answer to number three: there are six people still on the bus—counting you, the driver, and your five passengers. And the answer to question number two? Count them; the bus made six stops.

Most people get only one right. They've spent all their energies keeping track of the on-and-off, so they can tell you how many people are still on the bus. But many miss even that one, because they forget to count the driver. Try the story on your friends, and see if one of them can make up a similar story, or a variation on this one, to test *you.*

It's fun and it helps develop the powers of concentration and listening that are so essential to improving the memory.

You can create your own memory tests; you can also make up tests for observation and awareness. And you can teach others, too. In fact, for the name game, you ought to teach your friends, your family, or your fellow club members first. Let them in on the basic techniques for remembering as I've taught them to you in this book. Never forget: The best way to learn something is to teach it, and this kind of practice helps sharpen the memory.

THE SKYSCRAPER GAME

That same philosophy is why I recommend this final game as a good exercise for improving the memory. This one requires you to build the highest linked stack you possibly can. Everyone playing the game must, of course, know the essentials of the stack-and-link system. Explain the importance of making concrete words of the ideas, and the need for visualizing colorful, absurd, exaggerated pictures. Stress the need for the individual to *see himself* in the picture he creates for the association. Remind everyone that the linking of each object to the others in the stack has to be strong and vivid. Each picture should affect those it's linked with through motion and action. And of course what makes the whole thing memorable is a willingness to use *the ridiculous* to link items together.

When everyone's ready, you or someone you choose should be given a dictionary, a magazine or a picture book. That person is the teacher, whose responsibility is to describe one concrete, tangible object at a time, allowing a few seconds for the participants to do their visualizing and linking. It's not necessary, or even wise, for the teacher to load beginners with a lot of details about the objects. Keep the list short and simple. Use ten items at first. Then try twenty. Then let the class graduate to thirty items. Eventually see if you or someone else can remember as many as a hundred items.

Your first list could include a radio, a TV set, a cow, a chair, a car, a house, a chicken, a pair of shoes, a wristwatch, and a typewriter—ten objects with no more details than I've just given here. And remember, don't snap them out too fast! Take your time. Allow everyone enough time between items to form strong pictures. Later, when they've all got the knack of it, you can add details and move it along faster—for example, a red Cadillac convertible with white sidewall tires, a pair of shoes with big purple bows, a typewriter with solid gold keys. People will surprise themselves at how well they recall the details, as well as the main object. It's easy once they get the idea and once they develop some positive habits for remembering things. It's possible for anyone who really wants to, and who really tries, to master these methods. Tell them that—and then let them prove it to themselves.

PRACTICE CAN BE FUN

There are many times when you can practice your own memory exercises. Any time you're in a car, a cab, a bus, a plane, or while you're waiting for someone to show up, you can practice any of the association techniques. Next time you travel, if there's someone with you, take turns giving each other a list of items for stacking. Whoever gives the list should write it down so there's no doubt about whether the Cadillac was red or blue.

Again, success in the art of memory can only be yours if you *practice*. And the best practice is to teach others. Start by teaching the whole family. You can let them read this book, and then go over it with them. If *you* do the teaching *yourself*, you'll learn a lot faster, and so will they.

It's been a lot of fun sharing my methods with you. They've helped my own memory, and I know they've worked for those I've taught over the years. All the methods will be easy to use if you work hard at learning and practicing them. Master them now, and you'll be able to use them throughout your life.

I feel as Ralph Waldo Emerson felt about teaching. He said: "The best service one person can render another person, is to help him help himself." I've loved helping you, and I know you'll do well!

Finally: remember to practice! And good luck!

Your Personal Memory Worksheet

Your Personal Memory Worksheet

Your Personal Memory Worksheet

Your Personal Memory Worksheet